Morning to Motivation

Practical Inspiration to Jump Start Your Day

Dar'shun
Kendrick

outskirts
press

"From Morning to Motivation"
#DarshunSpeaks about her morning
motivations on life and business

Table of Contents

Foreword

"I knew my friend Dar'shun was an accomplished attorney and elected official, but what I didn't know is that she is also an accomplished author. Having grown up in the same neighborhood as Dar'shun, I am proud to know that she has put her childhood experiences and life lessons (so far) on paper to share with and inspire the world. I can tell you that I was inspired by her stories and "call to action" to develop myself personally and professionally. As a broadcaster, professor and entrepreneur, I understand the power of information. You WILL NOT be disappointed by this book and what she has to say."

-Dr. Rashad Richey, Professor/Radio Talk Show Host/ Author & Editor

Author Biography

Dar'shun Kendrick is a corporate securities lawyer, an investment adviser, a blogger on professional and personal topics of inspiration, and a member of the Georgia House of Representatives. She has dedicated her life to inspiring others to become their best selves, advocating for racial economic equity and wealth building. She was born and raised in Georgia by her parents, who taught her the value of faith, love and dedication to being my best self. In addition to serving as an elected official, she currently runs a law and investment advisory firm, a personal branding firm and a real estate syndication and investment group. She enjoys cooking international foods and trying new recipes as well as and playing with her dog Dezzy at their home in Lithonia, GA.

Preamble- My 2021 Morning Affirmations

Today, I will find a way to tell someone about the GOODNESS of the Lord.

Today, I will find a way to BUILD black wealth.

Today, I will EXPECT God to do exceedingly, abundantly above all that I can ask or think.

Today, I will live life WITHOUT fear or regret and EMBRACE opportunities, including the ones that scare me.

Today, I will LOVE and SERVE others sacrificially.

Today, I will not give anyone or anything my JOY or PEACE.

I cannot say "thank you" enough to:

- My God
- My Parents & family
- My Friends
- My community, including my Transforming Faith Church family

Introduction/
How to Use This Book

I never thought I would write a book. But I also never thought I would have my own law firm, or be elected to the Georgia legislature at the age of 27. Like so many things in my life, I never planned on becoming an author—but life has ways of showing you how to best use your talents. Who knew that this shy girl from a low-income family in Decatur, GA("known to Georgians as "the Dec") would become a highly demanded corporate lawyer, a registered investment advisor, a leader in the Georgia House of Representatives, a public speaker and an author ---when NONE of her 4 grandparents even obtained their high school diploma? THAT is a book and a praise dance ALL by itself!

This book is meant to be read a few minutes each morning of the work week for a full year. On Saturday and Sunday, I challenge you to find your own ways to be inspired. I strongly encourage you to read AND reflect on each section, internalizing what is being said and finding ways to apply it to your life THAT DAY. Passages are intentionally short to provide time to read and reflect on the given principles. This book includes stories, mini-sermons, affirmations to speak aloud and internalize, as well as "action items" on how to implement weekly lessons. Like most things in life, you will only get out of this book what you put into it, so I encourage you to read daily and find a way to apply it to your life.

I made a conscious decision to write this book because I have been told that I inspire people to be their best selves---- quite a compliment given the trials and tribulations I have encountered in my own life. And it's a compliment that I don't take lightly! So, I decided to put my thoughts on paper in the hopes that I can inspire more people in their personal, professional, and spiritual lives. Enjoy, and follow & connect with me on social media and subscribe to my blog. You can find the links on www.DarshunSpeaks.com.

If you don't speak over your life, someone else will.

My morning routine (See appendix)

I believe that our words put energy out into our thoughts and actions, good or bad. I also believe that we don't have to be the ones doing the talking to put out that energy. That's why every morning I say 6 positive affirmations for my day

Preamble- My 2021 Morning Affirmations

Today, I will find a way to tell someone about the GOODNESS of the Lord.

Today, I will find a way to BUILD black wealth.

Today, I will EXPECT God to do exceedingly, abundantly above all that I can ask or think.

Today, I will live life WITHOUT fear or regret and EMBRACE opportunities, including the ones that scare me.

Today, I will LOVE and SERVE others sacrificially.

Today, I will not give anyone or anything my JOY or PEACE.

Because you see---no one needs to be speaking what should be happening over my life without me speaking over it as well. And if I don't start speaking over your life, I assure you others will, and you may not like what they say.

Tales from the Dec

My mom often tells me the story of what happened when I was around 9 months old I was a newborn and my parents had gone to the grocery store. As they were exiting the car, a man asked if he could pray over me. My mom gave the man the side eye; my dad, being the nice person he is, apparently agreed to this random prayer by this random man. Long story short, the man prayed that I would be special and impact the world one day. My parents had already spoken that into my life, but they were happy for the confirmation---no matter how random the circumstances.

If you don't speak over your life, someone else will.

REPEAT AFTER ME (3 TIMES): <u>I am enough. I have</u> <u>what I need to attain my heart's desires and become</u> <u>all that I have been created to be. I. am. Enough.</u>

Q & A with DK

Q: When did you start the routine of doing positive affirmations each morning?

A: I don't think there was an *"a-ha moment"* when I started doing positive affirmations. I can re-member as a teenager writing down inspirational quotes on index cards and keeping them in a box. Like so many people, I am a very visual person--things become real when I see them in writing (guess that's why I am a lawyer, right?) And like so many people, I need inspiration every day be-cause life happens, and I have big things planned to do in my short time on Earth. Even now, my house is filled with sticky notes and pictures with positive quotes so when things get rough, I have constant reminders to help me through.

"Call to Action" (Fill in the blank): Write down 4-6 positive things you want to manifest in your life. Make them short, so they are easy to remember and try ot encompass who you are as a person and what you are passionate about in life. Hang them in places you frequent throughout the day. When you see them, re-cite aloud until you have them memorized. BONUS:

Commit them to memory and recite them every morning. Watch the transformation in your thinking and behavior!

Today, _____

Today, _____

Today, _____

Today, _____

Today, _____

99 ½% won't do.

All or nothing

There is a song "All or Nothing" on the soundtrack of one of my favorite movies, "Save the Last Dance", that really sums up how I feel about giving my ALL to anything I do---big or small---paid or unpaid. The words of the song from Athena say *"From your fears, you have to wean yourself. It's all or nothing---give your everything."* If you are going to do something, particularly something that scares you, why would you give it anything less than 100%? Not committing 100% to your passion is one of life's greatest travesties. Because at the end of the day, you don't want to fail because you only gave 80% or 90% of even 95%. Go all-in to improve your chance of success.

Tales from the Dec

My mom raised all three of us Kendrick kids on gospel songs---Shirley Caesar, Al Green, every community mass choir in the land; they were the royalty of gospel music back in the day. I remember a song I heard as a teenager by a gospel choir that said, *"Lord I'm running---trying to make 100---because 99...and a half... won't do."* The song was about our spiritual relationship with God, but the same words can be applied to everything we do in life. We must start with the mindset that even 99 ½% won't do.

REPEAT AFTER ME (3 TIMES): <u>Whatever I decide to do, I will give it 100%. Not 80, 90 or 99 ½---only 100% will do.</u>

Q & A with DK

Q: It seems that music influenced or spoke to your belief in giving 100% in all that you do, but surely your ubpringing played a part as well?

A: It did absolutely! My mom specifically influenced and reinforced this personal mantra of giving anything I say "yes" to 100% and nothing less. I remember her telling me to vacuum the floor, and as most kids often did, I tried to vacuum around the furniture, not wanting to take the effort to move it. But when she returned to make sure I had done my chores correctly, she discovered I'd attempted to get away with doing only half the job. She ended her lecture to me with the following advice, and it's always stuck with me: *"If you are going to do something, do it 100% or not at all."*

"Call to action"- I believe one of the reasons we don't give 100% to something is because we may be over-stretched in time or resources, or we aren't quite as passionate about the task as we ought to be. Narrow down what you choose to take on, so you can give 100% to a few things that matter, and not 80% to 20 things that may not. Answer the following questions:

1.   What projects or organizations am I truly passionate about?
2.   What projects or organizations do I truly have time for?
3.   What projects or organizations fit BOTH of these descriptions?

Eliminate/downsize the rest.

Live life because others can't.

My best childhood friend

April of 2018, my life changed forever. I received a text message from my mom that said my best childhood friend of over 25 years had died. She had been in the hospital for a while and, honestly, we were not speaking at the time she passed. There was a miscommunication about a post I made on social media that my friend assumed was about her. Talk about guilt AND sadness all at once! But in that utter despair, I asked myself what my friend would want me to do about living life and it was this: Live life. She was the spontaneous one in our childhood group—full of life and excitement and love. In her death, she taught me to live life more, and I will be eternally grateful for that lesson. We all have loved ones who are no longer here. Make it a point to live in their memory.

Tales from the Dec

When I say "live life", which to me means living life without regrets and taking risks, of course I mean in moderation and within means. We must plan for our futures, we can't be out here "living la vida loca" all the time. Case and point: Senior skip day at Towers High School. Did I skip? Yes. Did I also ask my mom if I could? Yes. I know---asking was seriously lame, but I figured I could either live life for senior skip day and face Daisy Kendrick at home---and have my life cut short----or I could ask permission and see what happens. It all worked out, and I lived to tell.

REPEAT AFTER ME (3 TIMES): <u>Today, I will be thankful. I commit to living my BEST life because someone else can't because they have moved from this life.</u>

Q & A with DK

Q: How have you started to live life more since your childhood best friend's untimely death?

A: Well, first I'll say that I am a work in progress, so I still don't possess half of the passion for life my friend once had, but I am working on my spontaneity, because as you can probably guess, I plan my days in 30 minute increments and they are filled from 5 am until about 7 pm. HOWEVER, if there is an opportunity to do something fun, I am likely to take it; saing "yes" to having fun was almost non-existent before my friend's death. For example, for my last birthday, a friend and I went to Hilton Head and spent four days shopping and eating and lying on the beach. I can assure you, five years ago that would NOT have even been an option. I would have found a way to work during my birthday.

"Call to action"

Write "I will live life because (fill in name) can't" on a sticky note and leave it somewhere you'll see it daily. Every time you are tempted to ignore an opportunity or work that extra hour instead of spending time with those you love, look at it---and remember.

Every day is a new opportunity.

There are forces working against your opportunity

I am absolutely convinced that one of the most deceitful tricks is someone is convincing us that evil doesn't exist or looks differently than we expect. I call it "The Great Deception," because I believe there are powerful forces working against us in life, even if we cannot see or feel them. The first step towards realizing you have hope and a promising future is to recognize there are forces trying to keep you in your past---by bringing up the bad parts of the past, reminding you of your bad parts of your past, giving you anxiety about your past that you want to forget. It's only then we can equip ourselves adequately to move forward and to realize that every day is a NEW opportunity to become our best self---Every. Single. Day.

Tales from the DEC

As a teenager, I heard a saying that said, "Every day is a gift from God; that's why it's called the present." What really struck me about this saying was the early realization that there are things I can change and others I cannot. I was pulled out of a school I liked going into my 5th grade year and taken to a school where I had no friends or connections. After rebelling for about a year and getting into all sorts of trouble, it finally dawned on me that I couldn't change my circumstances. I was stuck there. So, I decided every day was a new opportunity to make new friends and new relationships with teachers---I accomplished the latter; not so much the former but more about that later.

REPEAT AFTER ME (3 TIMES): Today is a new day---filled with new opportunities and challenges that I know I can handle. Today is a new and glorious day—and I will take advantage of the opportunities in front of me!

Q & A with DK

Q: What do you have to say to a person in difficult circumstances long term who doesn't see every day as a new opportunity, but rather just another day of heartache and grief?

A: First, I say: I understand. 2018 was the worst YEAR of my life, which I will detail in a subsequent book.

Every day I woke up, there was something different and horrible going on. I didn't know when it would end. But I remembered that each day was moving toward a time when my grief would end. Everything goes in cycles—so count the days going forward. Change the narrative in your mind and look for the positive in each day. You are that much closer to a breakthrough and ending this situation." It will give you hope for future days.

"Call to Action"

Today is a new day to _____. The past is behind me and my future is in front of me. Today is a great day to _____ (same from 1st sentence.) Print. Hang. Recite. Do.

It's ok to be picky with your network.

You are who you hang around

Ha! I sound like my parents when I was growing up. But it's true----the older I get, the more I see it. The book "The Energy Bus" by Jon Gordon described life as a bus. Who we allow on our bus and what seats we give away determine how we meet our destiny. Some people get on for a few stops and then voluntarily get off. Some get on without paying, and think they are going to ride to your destiny, so you must kick them off. Some people think they are going to sit in the driver's seat, your seat, and drive the bus! Knowing who to let in your life is particularly important. It's never too late to re-evaluate and make changes.

Tales from the DEC

Remember when cell phones were fairly new? You could choose your top 5 people to call without using your minutes. (Remember when we had a certain number of minutes? These Generation Z kids will NEVER know struggle.) I remember thinking seriously about who would be in my top 5. My parents were there of course, but the other 3 slots I took some thought. Who did I want to give the privilege of being in those slots? Eventually it came down to my boyfriend at the time, my job, and my best friend; because at the time, they were the priorities in my life. If I had a choice today, those three remaining slots may be different. That's how it's supposed to be. When we change, so do priorities.

REPEAT AFTER ME (3 TIMES): <u>I am in control of my circle of influence. Today and every day, I choose those on the same track as my own---and I make NO apologies about it!</u>

Q & A with DK

Q: Being selective with your network can be hard, particularly for people who are naturally friendly or extroverted, or those trying to start a business where relationships matter. How do you balance all that?

A: Well first, I am not an extrovert so that helps. I never had many friends in school and was bullied endlessly. But that experience taught me more than ever that I must be careful of who I hang around. I want people that genuinely like me. When I say be selective, I am not saying don't be friendly or don't take that coffee meeting to generate business---I am telling you to choose people that have the most positive impact on your life.

"Call to Action"

List the five (5) people you hang around the most (outside of immediate family) then list their good and bad characteristics. Do they reflect your own? If not, you can always switch up your top five (5).

Never take "no" for an answer.

"No" just means 'try again"

Everyone should get used to hearing "no" in life and in business. It's going to happen, possibly several times, but all you need is one "yes" to turn things around. So how to you get that "yes" you ask? Keep trying. "No" is not final. "No" is not your destination. "No" does not give you an excuse to give up. All it means is that "yes" might take a little longer than you expected. But you are that much closer, so roll up your sleeves, get over the "no," and ask again.

Tales from the DEC

In high school, I was a part of Girls State, a program that invited young girls from all over Georgia to participate in mock elections and grow their understandings of how government works. Only two girls were chosen from each high school, with preference for those with family serving in the military. At the time, my school already had two exceptional female students whose family members had served. I really wanted to go, so I contacted the organizers and made the case for why I should be chosen. And for the first time in Girls State history (I am told), they chose three girls from my high school as representatives. I realized then that if I wanted something bad enough, I improved my chances of success if I kept trying.

REPEAT AFTER ME (3 TIMES): <u>"No" is not final. It just means I need to try again.</u>

Q & A with DK

Q: This concept sounds like something that you learned as a child---this concept of never taking "no" for an answer. Tell us about that.

A: My mom would always tell us, "If someone tells you "no," ask to speak to their supervisor. If they say "no," ask to speak to THEIR supervisor, until you get to the top. And even then, "no" doesn't necessarily mean "no." She was right, like with most things. Some of our greatest businesspeople were told "no" multiple times before they heard a "yes." What separates successful entrepreneurs from unsuccessful ones is tenacity and perseverance---not money, not connections, not fame, but the ability to keep going when things aren't going as planned.

"Call to Action"

Think about the last person who told you "no". Were they the highest authority? I DARE you to go back to the situation and ask again, and if they say "no" ---ask to speak to someone above them.

Learning is a marathon, never a sprint.

4 degrees, 2 licenses and 2 certificates later.

I know what you're probably thinking. And yes, I may be an overachiever but honestly, I just like learning: pure and simple. I didn't and don't need 4 degrees, 2 licenses and 2 certifications to do most of what I do, but the things I was interested in provided these things, so here we are. You don't need to be a professional student like me, collecting degrees and student loan debt in order to become all God has called you to be. You can do something each day to improve your skills or learn something new. Each of us can do this by setting aside time in our schedules to read or watch things that add to our knowledge base. When we stop learning, we stop growing.

Tales from the DEC

My mom is the epitome of a persistent woman. She required, not asked, but REQUIRED only As and Bs in her household. Even when I brought home low Bs, she gave me a cautious eye that told me to do better. My momgenuinely believed that education was the way we were going to be successful in life and low "Bs" were too close to being "Cs" for her liking. We were allowed one (1) hour of TV per day, and the rest were dedicated to reading or doing homework. At the time, I thought she was a mean mom depriving me of fun, but now I realize---she knew in unsophisticated terms that education was the great equalizer in the world that was going to bring this girl from Glenwood Road so many opportunities. She was right, and I am eternally grateful for this habit she formed in me at an early age.

REPEAT AFTER ME (3 TIMES): <u>I will be a lifelong learner. Every day I will learn SOMETHING new and never accept I have learned all I can.</u>

Q & A with DK

Q: Where can people find time to learn? I think most people believe their learning days are over once they graduate, so how do you incorporate learning into your busy life?

A: I believe that you can find time for things that are priorities---period. We all get 24 hours a day, how we use that time makes all the difference. I literally schedule time to learn—1 hour a day— the same way I schedule meetings or fun outings. I schedule my learning time and I am disciplined enough to stick to it NO MATTER WHAT. You must make it a mandatory activity. It can be French lessons or reading a book or attending a webinar. Pick whatever works for you, but be intentional about it or the day can and will get away from you.

"Call to Action"

1. What is something you want to know more about? (It can be something that develops you professionally, or maybe something as simple as learning how to cook international dishes.

2. Write down what you want to learn over the course of a year, and be specific. (For example, I want to learn how to build a sophisticated excel model for cash flow projections.)

3. Break down your yearly goal into smaller monthly, weekly, and daily goals.

4. Write your daily goal on a sticky note or add it to your calendar.

5. Stick to it. Repeat.

Represent others well.

My parents

You will notice throughout this book that I mention my parents consistently. It's because parents usually are the greatest influence of our lives, good or bad, and luckily God blessed me with the best parents I could ever want. Of course, I didn't realize it as a kid and didn't understand why my parents did what they did. But I do now, and I am eternally grateful. They inspire me to be the best version of myself. I make sure I represent them in public and private as they raised me. We all have those people or things that inspire us to be better. Let's reflect them in our actions, and particularly in how we treat others.

Tales from the DEC

By now you know that I have a black momma, so for those of you with black mommas, I'm sure this won't come as a surprise: When I was growing up, my mom would say "You embarrass me, I am going to embarrass you." as a general phrase to warn us Kendrick kids not to act up in public. —and I could tell she meant it! If we were dropped off somewhere, we knew we had be on our best behavior, because if word got back to her that we acted outside of how she raised us, we were in for it! Big time! The reason she required us to behave even outside of her presence was because we reflected who she was and how we were being raised. We understood that no matter if she was in our presence or not, we represented Daisy and Ricky Kendrick, and we were to do so well.

REPEAT AFTER ME (3 TIMES): <u>How I behave is a reflection of those I am associated with and therefore, I will represent others to the best of my ability---in all ways, at all times, to all people.</u>

Q & A with DK

Q: How has what your parents taught you about representing them transferred into your adult life?

A: Well obviously as an attorney who literally represents clients, I make sure that in any transaction— particularly with someone on the other side of a deal— I am representing my client in the best light possible. It's what they deserve and expect, because who they choose for representation in legal matters is an assessment of my client's character.

I carry the same attitude as an elected official. People took their sacred vote and entrusted it with me and stated with their vote that they trust me to represent them in the best possible way. I have an obligation to represent them well, so it reflects well on the entire district that they know how to choose leaders.

"Call to Action"

Think about all the people you represent in your job and in life. Are you reflecting the best version of your community to the outside world knowing you represent it? If not, it's not too late to change. Because at the end of the day, there's the Golden Rule: Treat others like you would like to be treated. How would you want someone to represent you?

Do "it" well or not at all.

LL Cool J

So, LL Cool J had a song called "Doing it well" ----
and yes it was NOT talking about what I am talking
about, the concept is still the same. If you are going
to do anything, do it well or not at all. I once heard it
said that : *"What you do, do well. What you don't do
well, don't do."* Think about that in both a personal
and professional context; that's the mantra to live by.
I am either going to go all-in and do my absolute
best or not at all. It underscores what my mom taught
me about giving anything I take on my all. It's that
simple.

Tales from the DEC

I play the violin, but I could also play the bass, viola
and cello if I wanted to. I started out on the bass in 6th
grade at Glenhaven Elementary with Dr. Coochie (se-
riously---that was his name. No wonder I got bullied.

Anyone who was given lessons by him was automatically associated with his name and made a laughing stock of the school.) I was in an orchestra with a handful of other kids. You had to practice —obviously— to learn to play these instruments. But sometimes, you know, I just didn't want to. I can still hear my mom's voice say, "Either you are going to learn to play this instrument or not at all." Which meant she was not going to let me play it at all. And so, she made me practice, which I am sure came at a great sacrifice to her because it wasn't like I was terribly good. I had tried to play other instruments like drums and didn't have enough wind or patience to play any instrument that required my lungs so I knew violin was the best I could do. Long story short: I still play when I can to this day, because it turned out I loved playing these instruments.

REPEAT AFTER ME (3 TIMES): <u>What I do, I do well— or not at all.</u>

Q & A with DK

Q: I think most people want to be able to do something well but because of lack of resources they cannot. What's your advice to people in those circumstances?

A: Every situation is unique and must be assessed on a case by case basis. For example, the single mom trying to raise kids and work several jobs. I know she may feel like she is barely raising her kids because she has to also put food on the table. So "well" is relative based on your abilities and circumstances. Like my mom always told me growing up, "All I ask is that you do your best." So, if your best is working 60 hours to keep food on the table and spending less than ideal time with your kids, that is doing it well—because that's your best. It's the same with startup entrepreneurs—In my business, I have had to be the CEO and janitor, the secretary and the accountant, so I understand there are obstacles to doing things well As long as you know in your heart you are doing your best, you are doing what you are doing well.

"Call to Action"

What I do well	What I don't do well	Assessment: The things you do well, how can you highlight and develop those talents? The things you don't do well, how can you give them to others to do well?

Get you a Joshua, Moses.

My "Girlfriends"

One of my favorite sitcoms of all time is "Girlfriends."
I really enjoyed the writing and the characters and the
real-world issues on that show. But what I got most
out of it was how real each of the characters were
with one another—telling each other the truth and
falling out (like when Joan wouldn't speak to Toni because she tried to sleep with her man) and then getting
back on track again. Even with all that, they had each
other's backs no matter what. We all need girlfriends/
homeboys like that in our lives where we can be honest with each other as much as possible without being
offended; and even if we are offended, we eventually
get back together because we need those people in
our lives to move forward.

Tales from the DEC

I grew up in the church and had two good friends that attended with me. We went to Sunday school together, went through high school together, got our first boyfriends, cars, and felt heartbreak together—my "ride or die" girls. During my preteen years, I thought I had a boyfriend, but apparently I didn't, because he was dating someone else. One day after church service, my two girlfriends found this out and confronted "the other woman" (who was like 12 by the way so none of this makes sense.) I didn't do any talking---they it did all for me. It was a glorious moment, I must say. I knew they were my true friends —they fought for me when I was too broken to fight for myself. And it made me think about our Sunday school classes and it hit me---these were my Joshuas (even if I was not a Moses). For those of you that don't already know the story, Moses let the children of Isreal out of Egypt and Joshua was Moses' right hand man and succeeded him after Moses' death.

REPEAT AFTER ME (3 TIMES): <u>I will appreciate those who are honest and who uplift me when I need it, and if I don't have any such friends, I will find some.</u>

Q & A with DK

Q: The title of this chapter seems Biblical in nature. Explain the name and the spiritual implications for what you are trying to tell readers.

A: Joshua was one of the leaders under the direction of Moses, tasked with leading the people of Israel out of captivity in Egypt and into the promised land. Joshua was responsible for following the direction of Moses but more than that, he was Moses' best and most fervent defender when the people of Egypt started doubting God's faithfulness to have Moses lead them to their destiny. In life, we need people who are going to encourage us, defend us and hold us accountable for where we are going in life. But I will also add: We not only need a Joshua in our life; we need to BE a Joshua as well. It's not one-sided.

"Call to Action"

Write down the "Joshuas" in your life—those who are true friends. Are you being a Joshua back to them? If not, how can you begin? Take that first step today.

Fear is everyone's Achilles heel.

Ask to make the announcements Nikki.

Black mommas are psychic. There, I said it. My mom knew that I was very introverted in high school, particularly because I was bullied so much, and so she was insistent---insistent ya'll---on making me step outside my comfort zone. She must have known that I would one day be on a national stage even if I never thought I could be because of my shyness. Every morning she would say "Why don't you ask if you can do the announcements on the intercom?" I was scared. *What if they say no?* I thought. *Or what if they say yes and I mess up a word or something and everyone hates me?* Keep in mind I was already highly unpopular. I never asked to make announcements, but I did do something else.

Tales from the DEC

It was my 11th grade year in high school when it happened— an open, appointed position for our student government's Spirit & Pride Chair. Because I was so unpopular, I couldn't actually win when I ran for an elected position so I had to get appointed to a student government position by someone who recognized my greatness. But I still had to go through an interview process and, ladies and gentlemen, the fear of speaking to ANYONE was terrifying. But I mustered up my courage to apply and sit through the interview with Brandy, the Student Body President, and guess what— I got the position and served as Spirit and Pride Chair for 2 years. It's small steps, y'all, that lead to big steps.

REPEAT AFTER ME (3 TIMES): Fear is the opposite of faith and both take the same energy. Therefore, I choose to spend my energy on faith and not fear.

Q & A with DK

Q: How important is it to take small steps to get over our fears and not think we must take one huge leap?

A: Did you know it takes the same amount of energy to fear something as it does to exercise faith and DO something you fear? Therefore, it's vitally important to take the first step, no matter how small, to overcome your fear. As the old saying goes "How do you eat an elephant? One bite at a time." We must take small steps to increase our faith and stride longer with the next step and continue. That small step of getting over my fear of rejection in high school was the catalyst for me being able to say "yes" when asked to run for the Georgia House of Representatives at the age of 27. If I were in the same fearful position as I was in the 11th grade, there would have been NO WAY I would have made such a daring and public endeavor. No way at all. Now, it seems, you cannot stop me from talking. Go figure.

"Call to Action"

Take out a dry erase board or a large sticky pad. Write down all your fears—big or small. Beside it, write WHY you are fearful. Now think about your life 10 years from now and ask if the reason why you are fearful will even matter. If not, I suggest you get to work! Fear can be paralyzing, but not as much as regret.

Smiling is good for you.

Tell your mind what to do.

It takes more muscles to frown than it does to smile. Did you know that? Not sure why I know that, but I do. But that random fact is deeper than you think: It tells me that negativity takes more WORK than positivity. And I am sure you are reading this saying "yeah, right" but if you think about it, when you are positive, there is a level of faith that everything is going to be ok. But when you are negative, if you are like me, you think about every possible negative scenario, how bad it could get, what to do at each stage of it worsening, and what the ultimate bottom you reach might be—that, ladies and gentlemen, is exhausting to think about! So yeah—it makes sense that it takes more work to frown than to smile, so smile ☺

Tales from the DEC

In school, I took a psychology and physiology class. It helped me realize that we are complex beings as far as our perception of reality being controlled by what we think, what we do or don't do, what our health and mental state are. But on a practical level, one of the most insightful things that I learned in that class was that we tell our mind what to do through unconscious, non-verbal cues. If we smile, it tells our brain we are happy. If we frown, it does the opposite. If we stand in a superman pose 30 minutes before an interview or test, studies show that we will perform better. We must constantly ask ourselves throughout the day—what are we telling our brains to think?

REPEAT AFTER ME (3 TIMES): <u>I will use every opportunity I can to smile and to tell my mind that everything is going to be ok.</u>

Q & A with DK

Q: How do you know which one you have been doing—frowning or smiling— more?

A: It's simple—I have laugh lines to prove it. There are distinct lines that form around our mouths as we get older called "laugh lines." I was in my mid-30s when I walked into a Macy's looking for some wrinkle cream (don't laugh.) The lady behind the counter asked why I was looking for wrinkle cream at my age and I told her I wanted to get rid of the laugh lines. I will never forget what she told me. "That is a testament to how happy you have been in life. You don't want to hide those." I left Macy's and have yet to try covering up my laugh lines again.

"Call to Action"

1. Stand in front of a mirror
2. Think about something that would normally worry you or make you sad.
3. Think about something positive about the situation even if it's that you are one day closer to bringing it all to an end
4. Instead of frowning, try looking at your expression when you think about the positive aspects of the situation
5. Does it improve your mood? Do you eventually smile, even if all you have now is a smirk?

The "Perspective" journey leads you.

Focusing on what we can control

Worrying is like a rocking chair: It will keep you busy, but you won't go anywhere. It's very true. Listen, life is filled with marble (good times) and mud (bad times.) Some things we can change, while others are out of our control. So, you know what I choose to do, particularly with the things I cannot change? I change my attitude and perspective. You may have heard it stated that 90% of life is not our situations but how we respond. It's easy to go through life bitter and angry and upset BUT life is VERY short ya'll—ain't nobody got time for that. Change your perspective and enjoy your short time on this Earth a lot more.

Tales from the DEC

In hindsight, I am convinced that I had a guardian angel with me in high school. The reason I think this is because I made it out of one of the lowest performing schools in the state of Georgia, which itself is at the bottom nationally as far as school performance is concerned. Our teen pregnancy rate seemed to increase the longer I was at the school. At the time, I was bullied and highly unpopular. For a teenage girl, that was devastating. Why didn't anyone like me? As I thought about what a black girl like me growing up in that neighborhood was expected to do, I realized my lack of popularity was God's protection from getting caught up in teen pregnancy and gun violence was going on at my high school at the time. I still was upset, but I always felt deep inside it was for a reason. And when I became an adult, I discovered that reason.

REPEAT AFTER ME (3 TIMES): <u>Some things I cannot control so instead I will control what I can—my response and my attitude.</u>

Q & A with DK

Q: How do you find positive perspectives in the middle of chaos and hardship? It's a nice thing to say we should do, but how you do actually do it?

A: I don't want to give the impression that it's always easy to find positive perspectives because there are people going through some seriously hard times. But my advice is to sit quietly, wipe away the negative parts of your situation and focus on whatever glimmer of positivity there might be— no matter how small it is. Take some time to really concentrate on that aspect of your situation really focus on that positivity. I am a big believer that we become what we focus on. So, focusing on the positive has to eventually influence my thoughts which in turn influence my actions. The goal is to find a positive perspective for your situation so that it's easier to bear. It won't solve your problem or make you happy, but it's imperative to find some glimmer of hope to give you the strength to fight and carry on.

"Call to Action"- Print this and stick somewhere.

I cannot control what happens to me, but I can control how I react. 90% of how a situation is handled is based on my reaction.

Remember the Golden Rule for yourself and others.

How do you want to be treated?

You have heard of the Golden Rule before- *Treat others like you want to be treated.* No matter your background or religious belief, most people believe this to be true. I want to extend that notion to you. Remember, that golden rule applies not only to your but to others as well. As we discussed before, who you hang around will affect you—even if you don't notice it immediately or want to admit it. So, this golden rule should not only be a requirement for yourself and your actions but others you bring onto your "life bus" as well. They reflect you as a person, and if they treat others poorly, you may find yourself doing similar actions eventually.

Tales from the DEC

Growing up, the Kendrick kids spent a lot of time at church. One day my little brother—the youngest of the three of us— was playing in the parking lot of the church throwing rocks (apparently that's what little boys do.) Well, he threw a rock that hit another church member's car and shattered the windshield. I saw it play out in slow motion. There were very few people around and I don't think anyone noticed what had happened—except my dad who happened to be outside. My brother could have gotten away with it and my dad could have pretended like he didn't see it, but he didn't. He immediately told the owner of the vehicle and offered to pay for the windshield which was NOT cheap. He also made my little brother apologize. It taught me a vital lesson: even when no one is watching, you are still to live by the Golden rule and make others abide by it as well.

REPEAT AFTER ME (3 TIMES): <u>Each person I meet is a copy of myself. How I treat them is how I want others to treat me.</u>

Q & A with DK

Q: **Does the Golden rule apply even when people aren't applying it themselves? It can seem like those that abide by this rule can find themselves getting used and the world thinks of them as weak.**

A: Short answer, yes. For me, I believe what goes around comes around—good or bad—so I am not looking for a reward or approval from the world. To be clear, I am not talking about putting yourself in situations to be used or taken advantage of and using the Golden rule as an excuse to be mistreated. You can remove yourself from people and situations so you no longer have to be the one treating others well while you yourself are being used. But you have to make that choice. Do not diminish the usefulness and importance of the Golden rule because you keep putting yourself in situations you shouldn't be involved in.

"Call to Action"

1. Name a situation in which you didn't treat someone how you would wanted to be treated.
2. Can you make amends?
3. If not, how do you prevent this from happening again?

Time alone is time well spent.

My closet

For those of you raised in the church, you may have heard the elders talking about "the prayer closet." Well, I have a closet as well, one that I use to pray, think, meditate, talk to God, talk to myself, scream, etc. Now I live alone in a moderately sized house, so I can find solitude, in theory, anywhere in my home. The reason I choose my literal closet is because the space is all mine---no one else can enter the space. It's dark, so I can really concentrate on what I am doing. It's a dedicated space, so mentally my mind knows what to do whenever I am in it. I highly suggest you find YOUR space and time to spend alone to get into the mindset you need to take on life.

Tales from the DEC

Listen, you may not believe me, but I was QUITE the pre-teen and teenager. I honestly believe I spent about

60% of my teenage years in trouble and "on punishment," which meant being stuck in my room, unable to leave. I believe my parents knew that if they isolated me, I would have to concentrate on what it was that I had done (or had not done) and internalize and correct my mistakes. Little did they know, I liked being alone, but it did give me time to write and plot my life. I decided one day while on punishment that I wanted to become President of the United States (I can sense the irony in that.) There are all types of benefits to being in isolation and tuning out the world even if you are already introverted like me. Try it.

REPEAT AFTER ME (3 TIMES): <u>I will commit to 15 minutes of "me time" every day—no distractions, no worries, no one else—just me.</u>

Q & A with DK

Q: How do you decide what to do during your alone time in your closet?

A: Whatever is on my mind. It's that simple. Each day has its own set of challenges and issues. I take those issues and give myself time to talk, think, and pray about whatever that issue is. I also use my closet to give thanks for all that I have, because I know that I am blessed and have unique talents and abilities that I want and need to share with the world. So be careful not to make your "closet" your space for complaining—use it as a space to have a conversation and reflect on the good and bad.

"Call to Action"

Where is YOUR place that is inaccessible to anyone else and allows you to concentrate without distractions? If you have that place, what do you associate with that place? Is it happiness, joy, contentment, peace or something negative in which case you need to find a new hiding place? If you don't have a place free from distractions, do you think it's possible to find one?

Enjoy the valleys on your way to the mountain top.

Dancing in the rain

It's very true that tough situations don't last but tough people do. Life is what it is. We all know that good times don't last, and troubles are a constant. We cannot control 100% of what happens to us in life 100% of the time. Knowing that what goes up must come down and vice versa, it's not too hard to understand why I enjoy my valleys. I know that if I am in a valley of my life, the mountain is on the other side of the journey if I just KEEP GOING. Being an investment adviser, I always tell people "markets go up, markets go down, what goes down must go up and vice versa" so nothing is ever as good or as bad as it seems. Just wait and keep pressing forward.

Tales from the DEC

I have been transparent about how I was treated in high school, but I think this is the first time I have mentioned that I started high school in the 8th grade. That's right—I technically skipped middle school altogether because we didn't have a middle school in my community at the time. So, my 1st semester of high school, I wanted to get all As on my report card; not sure why since my mom accepted Bs, but I did. My 1st year of high school in the 8th grade, the bullying took on newer levels than in elementary school. It was a rough year, adjusting to being around older kids AND still being bullied. But let me tell you what, when I got all As and was just waiting on my A in Algebra, my teacher called me at home to tell me I had earned the grade and I felt everything I had gone through, even the constant bullying, was worth it. I decided then to enjoy my valleys on my way to my mountaintops because there will be valleys but mountaintops are on the horizon.

REPEAT AFTER ME (3 TIMES): <u>For every valley there is a mountain and for every mountain there is a valley. It's the cycle of life and I will learn to live in it.</u>

Q & A with DK

Q: Why would anyone want to ENJOY their valleys? Valleys are hard and depressing and make people

sad so explain WHY you enjoy your valleys so much—isn't it counterintuitive to human nature?

A: The simple answer is I believe that I am ON MY WAY to my mountaintop. I am a creature of habit and so I look at patterns as a predictor of future behavior. When I look back over my life, right before extraordinary blessings and breakthroughs I went through what seemed like hell right before. And so, based on that history, when I am going through valleys, I already know what's on the other side if I keep the faith and keep going. The key to getting out of the valley and to the mountaintop is to KEEP GOING and don't stop in the valley. The pattern has never let me down, so I know where I am going when I am in my valleys and so I can't help but anxiously anticipate and feel excited about what's to come. I had to train my mind to think this way—but it has worked.

"Call to Action"

Declare what you want to see on the other side of your valley. What does it look like? Who are you sharing it with? How do you savor the moment? How can you change your attitude with the expectation of what's on the other side of your valley?

Connect with something greater than yourself.

What is "something"?

When I say connect with something or someone greater than yourself, I don't mean to be spooky. This isn't meant to be a sermon on how to be religious or spiritual. However, I do think we all need to believe and connect with something greater than ourselves. Even for those that don't believe in a higher being necessarily, is there a mission, purpose or cause greater than you that you are willing to die for to keep intact? Having that connection to and knowledge of something bigger than us keeps us hopeful and striving towards our future. It also can be instrumental in guiding our morals and how we make decisions because there is something higher to support.

Tales from the DEC

In my thirties, I started telling people one of the greatest gifts my mom gave me was the gift of salvation at the age of 9 in a little brick building in Jonesboro, GA. I may have been too young to comprehend the entirety of what I was undertaking, but I appreciate those steps now more than ever. Even though I was young when I accepted Christ into my life and didn't understand the deeper spiritual guidelines of how to live a Christian life that was fulfilling and God centered, I understood that I had someone who was always with me and always wanted my best. For a bullied kid with big dreams, that was all I needed to know. It's served me well ever since, and I have been able to build on my relationship with Him who is greater than me. It gives me purpose and hope and guides my morality. I am thankful every day.

REPEAT AFTER ME (3 TIMES): <u>This day I connect to something or someone that's bigger than me---and I will continue to remember this as often as needed.</u>

Q & A with DK

Q: **Why is it so important to you to connect with something or someone bigger than yourself? I mean, this whole book is about motivating yourself so why do you need someone or something bigger to do that?**

A: Well obviously I cannot speak for anyone else BUT for me, it's important for me to have my God, who is much bigger than me, because when a huge dream is put into my heart (like this book) or when life gets hard—if all I have is myself to rely on, I am in trouble! I am human and I come with human characteristics like weakness, selfishness, lack of faith, etc. And as strong as I am all those human characteristics would eventually overtake me if I didn't cling to my faith and my God, some-one greater than me. THAT is why I connect ev-eryday with my God.

"Call to Action" (Fill in the blank)

_____ is bigger than me and so I will connect with _____ _____ every chance I get to strength-en, encourage and bring myself through the difficult circumstances in life but I also know connecting to _____ will empower me to be the best version of myself and accomplish my heart's desires.

Family cannot be replaced.

Kendrick?

There are more Kendricks in the world than you may think. Every now and again, I meet a Kendrick, or a Kendrick will inbox me on social media and ask, "Are we related"? And I answer "I don't know," because Kendrick is an adoptive name from my step grandfather. My mom was a foster kid and adopted so there is extraordinarily little I know about my biological family unfortunately. But the few Kendricks I do know are all mine. We have had some interesting times, but at the end of the day, you can choose your friends, but you can't choose biological family. They are what you are stuck with so I choose to embrace the family I have been placed in and to support them as much as I can.

Tales from the DEC

It was around Halloween and my younger brothers and I were collecting candy at our church as we normally did. At some point, the candy ran out and I was asked to share what I had collected with my two younger brothers. Now mind you, because I was the oldest and the only girl, I didn't have to share much. But I threw a fit because I had to share at all. But get this: I was willing to share with my friends at the time because, in my pre-teen mind my friends were a higher priority. As you can probably imagine, my parents gave me a lashing for it that really should go down in the history books. The gist of the hour-long lecture was this: Never let anything or anyone come between your own flesh and blood, not even best friends.

REPEAT AFTER ME (3 TIMES): <u>Family is all I have and was given specifically to me. I will embrace all their good and try to modify all their bad.</u>

Q & A with DK

Q: How does it make you feel, not knowing a lot about your biological family? Are you closer to the family you do know?

A: The interesting thing about me is that I thrive in smaller settings. It's the reason I choose a small liberal arts college even though I got into the University of GA and could have gone for free (my parents still think I am crazy for that one). So, the intimacy of my family doesn't bother me as much as you might think. I have friends with large families and there always seems to be drama, so I don't think I am missing that much—although that could totally be a false assumption. I do feel closer to the family I have, because it's a very small circle. What I do miss about knowing my family history is the medical portion of it: Every time I go to the doctor and they ask about family medical history, most of the paper is left blank or marked "unknown." We know how important family history is from a medical standpoint and that's going to be get more and more important as I get older, so I think about it every time I'm in a doctor's office.

"Call to Action"

I am going to call the following family members I haven't spoken to in at least six (6) months:

1. _____

2. _____

3. _____

4. _____

5. _____

Be a friend, gain a friend.

I have very few friends.

And it's totally my fault. I have a Type A personality and most experts will tell you that Type A personalities have a hard time making friends because we are so focused on our objectives and goals that we can trample people to reach them. Though the older I get, the more I want to cultivate relationships, because it seems pointless to conquer the world and have no one to share it with. So, these last three or so years I have been on a personal journey not to gain more friends, but to be a better friend to the ones I already have. I wonder how I am doing. I guess I will have to pick up the phone and ask.

Tales from the DEC

She stole my future boyfriend in the 10th grade. No, she didn't know I liked him and no he didn't know I liked him but that's not the point. I was intent on making this boy my boyfriend and one of my best friends got him because she was cuter than me. The teenage girl within me wanted to get mad and bitter, but luckily I had the foresight to see the vast universe of other eligible boys there were to choose from at my young age. I figured encouraging and supporting her relationship with my would-be boyfriend would pay dividends well into the future, unlike some rusty, old boy. I mean—I was only 15. And it did. We are still friends today!

REPEAT AFTER ME (3 TIMES): I cannot ask for a friend if I am unwilling to be a friend. Friendship is a reciprocal beneficial relationship.

Q & A with DK

Q: I think most people think "friend" has a very generic term which has been voided of all meaning because it's used so loosely nowadays. What do you look for in a friend?

A: For me, it's simple: Someone who likes me for all of my insecurities, vices and misfeasances. (I am notorious for not talking to friends for months at a time.) If you can accept me for who I am and understand I am truly a work in progress, that is what friendship means to me. Unless it's something harmful, I won't try to change you if you won't try to change me. But my personality is not for everyone and I understand and appreciate that. It's all good. There is someone for everyone, so I look for MY someones.

"Call to Action"

Think of your closest friends. What do they do to show that they are your friends? Calls, invitations, gifts? What do you do in return to show you are being a friend back? It doesn't have to be the same way. How do you show friendship, and can you do more of that?

Wars are won when battles are chosen.

Choose your battles wisely

Rule number one of human nature is self-preservation. So, whenever anyone dares to disagree or confront us, our first instant is to defend ourselves and our honor. But listen, just like everyone has 24 hours in a day, everyone has a limited amount of energy to expend each day before we need to rest and replenish. Therefore, I must ask myself how I will spend my 24 hours and how will I spend my energy—because both things are finite. The things that REALLY matter should be the only things that get both my time and energy.

Tales from the DEC

I think one of the things that maybe frustrates my mom the most is that I have always, even as a kid, known that some battles aren't worth fighting. My mom would lecture me on this or that and I would sit there with the most blank expression on my face. It would get her so mad. "Stop acting so nonchalant!" she would say. It wasn't that I didn't care, but I knew that the next week I would be in the same situation (I was quite the hard-headed kid,) so I figured *why fight it now? We are going to be in the same situation next week.* Not a very strategic thought process because I should have been thinking about correcting my behavior, but I was a teenager. The point is that I didn't devote time or energy to fighting to things that wouldn't make a difference in the long term.

REPEAT AFTER ME (3 TIMES): <u>Today, my energy will ONLY be spent on things that matter and things that I can change.</u>

Q & A with DK

Q: People understand that there is a finite amount of time and energy we can spend on life, good and bad; but the harder question is, how do you decide WHAT to spend that energy on when, at the moment in question, a particular issue does seem to matter?

A: Well remember the second part of the equation when deciding what to give your time and energy to is this: you must be able to change the situation. Arguing with someone you KNOW is not going to change their mind is a waste of time. Using your time and energy to correct a situation that you have NO control over is a waste of time. Period. Full stop. End of story. I know it's easy to think in the heat of the moment that THAT particular issue NEEDS to be addressed, but that's why it's important to develop the habit of subconsciously asking yourself if it matters in the long run and if can you do anything to change the situation.

"Call to Action"

Write a list of the last three (3) issues you can remember. Then go through the "2-part test" to see if they were worth the battle.

Issue No. 1: _____

1. Would this issue matter in 5 years?
2. Could you change the outcome?

Issue No. 2: _____

1. Would this issue matter in 5 years?
2. Could you change the outcome?

Issue No. 3: _____

1. Would this issue matter in 5 years?
2. Could you change the outcome?

Omnipotence is for the gods.

It's ok to say "I have no idea."

We all know those people—you know, the ones who walk around like they are God's gift to mankind. They act as if they can do no harm and know everything about, well, everything. They won't admit wrongdoings and have answers for everything. Most of us are wise enough to know that omnipotence is reserved for the gods, not man. So, it is ok to respond with the answer "I don't know" or "I have no idea." That way, no bad information is being given and you'll connect with rational people because they know no one has all the answers. We live in a world where it's looked down on not to seem like the smartest person in the room, but it's actually a showing of strength to admit you don't have all the answers. At least that's what I think.

Tales from the DEC

One of the many things I appreciate about my parents is the savvy way they raised us. While my mom required that I seek knowledge and learn continuously, it was ok not to know the answer to something. Now I *was* required to follow up and find the answer because she wasn't going to let me get off the hook, but the initial response of simply "I have no idea, mom," was a sufficient initial answer. I truly believe this helped me get comfortable with not having all the answers and not having to pretend to—but if you give me the chance, I can find out.

REPEAT AFTER ME (3 TIMES): <u>It's ok not to have all the answers, but I have the responsibility and ability to find them.</u>

Q & A with DK

Q: As a business owner who represents business owners, surely you can understand the fear of people saying "I don't know" or "I have no idea" in a corporate setting. To many, it makes you seem incompetent, and people are terrified of being judged or embarrassed.

A: Fair enough. It's one thing if you are preparing for something like a trial or a presentation and you don't know something—I can understand that pressure. So yes, absolutely prepare for something you know is coming your way. But even in those situations, would you rather give out bad information or be honest and say "I don't know but I will find out and get back with you"? At the end of the day, you don't know what you don't know. It is what it is. However, in situations that are less stressful, why are you trying to prove you know everything? Who are you doing this for? For me personally, I respect someone who tells me they don't have an answer but will find out, versus the person who has no idea what they are talking about but it just moving their lips to move them.

"Call to Action"

The next time someone asks you a question you don't know the answer to, say, "I don't know but I will find out." And the next one after that, and the next one, until it becomes habit.

Fail fast.

Failure is a part of success.

Sometimes I am utterly amazed when people inbox me to tell me I inspired them or helped them with a problem, because I think about what it took to get me here. All the heartaches and pain and difficult circumstances of my life have truly been a catalyst for keeping me inspired and inspiring others around me. I think about the messages I get and I think "if you only knew," but that's how it is, right? People see your mountaintops but never your valleys, people see your chapter 25 and never truly understand how rough it was in chapters 10-24, people see you as a diamond and forget that you had to be formed and made with the pressures of life. Remember, it's never a question of IF you fail but WHEN—failure is a requirement of success. How you deal with failure will make all the difference on your journey to success, so get it over with fast and bounce back even faster.

Tales from the DEC

In the Kendrick household, we didn't have a lot of crying. Why? Because we were taught that crying is good for a while but eventually, you must keep going on with life. Rather for me, it was going on with not getting elected to a study government position in school, not getting the grade I wanted or something else not working out the way I planned. My mom's attitude was that life goes on whether we are crying or weather we are fighting, and we should choose to continue fighting. I would start complaining and sobbing and my mom would say, quite bluntly, "Are you done?" When I think about it now, the way she said it was hilarious, but that woman taught me how to grow the tough skin I have now, and in life and politics, it has served me WELL! Fail fast and get on with it. Such a powerful lesson from my mom.

REPEAT AFTER ME (3 TIMES): <u>It's only a failure if I allow it to keep me from going forward. So, I will fail fast and bounce back even faster to keep moving forward.</u>

Q & A with DK

Q: What does "fast" mean to you? I can see where it means different things to different people.

A: For me it means what is proportionate to the type of failure and the next opportunity. You don't want to be wallowing in your failure while the next opportunity comes and goes and you missed it because you're still grieving about the last loss. So, for small things, I personally give myself a day to be sorrowful, maybe even only a few hours. For larger failures, I give myself a week of eating carbs and sweets, then I am done. Everyone has to do what works for them as "fast," because every person and situation is different, but the main lesson is to do what you must to grieve as quickly as possible so you can get up and keep moving towards your destiny.

"Call to Action"-
PRINT & HANG SOMEWHERE.

FAIL FAST.

Humility is a forced trait.

Pride comes before the fall

There is a Biblical principle that states that pride comes before the fall. I will be the first to admit that for overachievers (that means you because you are reading this book) it can be harder to display humility than most people. Admit it—we have done it all, seen it all, accomplished so many great things, that to admit we need help sometimes seems like we are being dishonest with ourselves. So, every now and then the universe recognizes this and brings some person or situation to knock us back down to human form and show us that either we must accept humility, or it will be forced upon us. Since I know that this is how God keeps me in check, these "knock down" moments are thankfully becoming less frequent the older I get. But not to worry! If ever I should become prideful in my own ability, I know there is a "knock down" moment around the corner just for me.

Tales from the DEC

As a kid, I knew I was smart. People told me I was smart, and I had the grades to prove it. I was Beta Club President, in the National Honor Society, President of the Debate Team, President of the DECA Club and President of the French club (yes—doing too much like I am doing as an adult.) So, when it was time to take the SATs, I thought "I got this. I'm smart." I wanted to go to Emory University in Atlanta. I didn't study—didn't take any prep classes—didn't ask advice from anyone. I just took the test cold turkey. And when I opened that envelope and saw I had gotten a 1080 out of the 1600 possible and the normal range for Emory applicants was around 1300—I got the wind knocked out of me. That is probably one of the most lasting lessons of my youth to remind me to never be so confident in myself that I think I don't need help.

REPEAT AFTER ME (3 TIMES): <u>I have accomplished many things but let me never get so proud as to forget that humility is a strength and a desired trait.</u>

Q & A with DK

Q: **I often think there is a fine line between humility and self-deprecation. So how do you toe the line between the two, particularly in situations that can get complex?**

A: I think of it in terms of how others perceive me. So, the goal is to have others do the work of telling me how I am perceived, right? I don't need to give myself compliments and neither do I need to openly criticize myself. So, if someone gives you a compliment, accept it without a qualifier. You are being humble because you didn't give yourself a compliment and you are not being self-deprecating because you accepted the complement fully and without a qualifier like "oh—I'm really not pretty" or, "no—the credit really goes to this person." In my example about my SATs, if I had made the effort to study for the test and someone else had said "You are super smart. You don't need to study," and then for some reason I decided to stop studying, I would have felt *less* like my pride had caused my downfall in my ability to master the SAT— which I eventually got up to an 1180.

"Call to Action"

1. The next time someone gives you a complement, just say thank you and be quiet. Women have a particularly hard time with this. Don't qualify the complement or try to make light of it or reroute the credit. Just say thank you and shut up.

2. The next time someone needs help with something that you think is trivial, offer help without thinking about why someone would need it.

3. Remember that we live in a country that allows for education of girls and the free exercise of our faith. In other countries, people are killed for either or both.

There is power in the pen.

Write the vision, make it plain

Studies have shown that you are much more likely to accomplish your goals if you write them down on paper. I will go a step further and say that the follow up to that is that you must put the written goals somewhere you can see them on a consistent basis. But this is something that I do daily, weekly, monthly, quarterly, and yearly. There are sticky notes EVERYWHERE throughout my home and office. But you can't just write them down, you have to check in with them to make sure you are progressing. It's not simply writing them that propels you towards your goals, but the reference to those goals to make sure you are holding yourself accountable for meeting benchmarks along the way. I told you I have a plethora of different size stickies in various colors all around me as a reminder of where I am going. It's not pretty, but it's effective.

Tales from the DEC

I had several journals when I was a teenager. Just random teenage thoughts. I also wrote a book of poetry and a futuristic book about me becoming the first female President of the United States. At the end of this book, I had an appendix detailing my entire political career from running for city council to my presidency. I gave a copy of this book to each of my favorite high school teachers. When I was first elected to the Georgia legislature in 2010, one of those teachers sent me that book and noted I was well on my way. There is POWER in writing things down and telling the universe what your ambitions are.

REPEAT AFTER ME (3 TIMES): I can accomplish my yearly goals if I work on them daily.

Q & A with DK

Q: Some goals are just so lofty and seem like too large of a task to accomplish. Any helpful tips for getting started and carrying through?

A: As the saying goes "How do you eat an elephant? One bite at a time." The most important thing is to GET STARTED. Once you get started, remember that the reason you break goals into benchmarks and tasks is because you're not expected to reach your goals overnight. So instead of trying to reach your yearly goal in 3 months when you know it will take a year, break it down to the daily micro targets and CONSISTENTLY and DILIGENTLY work towards that yearly goal. The goal is to do it consistently—our daily habits lead up to our yearly accomplishments.

"Call to Action"

1. Write down your yearly goals (3-5)
2. Break down those yearly goals into quarterly benchmarks.
3. Break down those quarterly benchmarks into monthly goals.
4. Break down those monthly goals into weekly targets.
5. Break down those weekly targets into daily micro goals.
6. Schedule a time daily to make sure you are meeting your daily micro goals.
7. At the end of each day, ask yourself if you have met your daily micro goals. If not, ask yourself why.
8. Check in weekly, monthly, quarterly, and yearly.

"No" is a verb.

And "no" is a complete sentence.

Luckily, I have always been firm that if I didn't want to do something, I just said no. People who know me will say you can bank on my word, because I mean what I say. That firmness comes from the fact that I completely understand what I am capable of but I also thoroughly understand and appreciate my limits. I think women have a particularly hard time internalizing that "no" is a complete sentence. You don't have to follow up with an explanation. Say "no" nicely and move on. Just like we can understand "yes" as a verb and action item, we can understand "no" as a verb and action item.

Tales from the DEC

I will admit that one of the reasons I was so unpopular in school was because I was short with people. I didn't mean to hurt people's feeling with how short my answers were but I saw it as a necessity. I have a personal belief that when people talk, they should be saying something that makes a difference and contributes to the conversaion. I don't understand people who talk just to hear themselves, so when I speak, I want my words to have some meaning. So I became notorious for rubbing people the wrong way, because when I was asked something, my only response was often "No." In hindsight, I could have finessed it a little and I apologize for that. I just believed in being straight with people without having to give a long explanation for my decision. I am better now at knowing when I need a follow up explanation and knowing how much of one to give.

REPEAT AFTER ME (3 TIMES): "No" doesn't always need an explanation or follow up. It is a complete sentence.

Q & A with DK

Q: Do you have a set of guiding principles in which you respond with just a "no"?

A: Well, they are extremely limited because now because in my line of work I cannot be too short, or it comes off as being very rude. But in general circumstances in which the gist of my answer is "no" is when I know that I am at capacity. From previous chapters hopefully what you have learned about me is that I like to do things 100%. If I know I cannot do something at 100%, my answer will be "no" to save my sanity and time and to save your sanity and time. As you can imagine, I get asked to do a lot of things. But I know I get asked out of respect for my work and talent and so my "nos" still mean "no" but I provide a short explanation that I hope is sufficient for the other party to understand. It works 99% of the time.

"Call to Action"

The next time you are tempted to say "yes" to something but really should say "no", say "no" then smile.

It's lonely at the bottom and the top.

.

Learn to be ok alone

I am still learning this. I will admit I am one of THOSE people that won't to go to the movies or out to eat or get my nails done alone. I want someone to talk to and share the experience with, BUT— if I want to do something and no one else is around, I have to do what I have to do. I mean, it's true that we were born into this world alone and naked and that's how we will die—at least the alone part! If you are like me and like to share your experiences, just know that you can also still have a good time by yourself. You may thrive better in smaller environments anyway. I felt that I was a much better law student than I was an MBA student because I was only accountable for my-self in law school, not relying on other people. In law school, you are taught to be competitive so working with other law students wasn't expected. So you see, sometimes being alone is not as bad as it seems.

Tales from the DEC

I am the first-born child and only girl in my family. So, I know a thing or two about being lonely. It never bothered me when I was younger because I never felt people understood me anyways. It was probably better that I had a semi-lonely existence growing up, because I was very introverted anyway so in being alone I found solace. But maybe it was preparing me for my life in general. I seem to thrive more when I am alone or with a very small group of friends than I do in crowds. I may not want to do fun things alone, but I know that if I have to, I can still enjoy it.

REPEAT AFTER ME (3 TIMES): <u>I don't have to share everything with anyone; I am enough.</u>

Q & A with DK

Q: Give an example of when you were alone and how it felt.

A: In 2013, I spent three days alone in Paris, France. I had two companions that were supposed to meet me there are didn't. In hindsight, it was the BEST time of my life and I am SO GLAD I didn't have people I was accountable for on the trip. I was able to decide my own schedule and it was magical. It was one of the BEST times of my life! Sometimes, we think we need people for things we don't. Being alone allows us to focus on the objective at hand without distraction.

"Call to Action"

I don't want to be alone because

_____

_____

_____

_____

_____

_____

_____

Community is everyone's calling.

We weren't made to be alone.

I know you are probably thinking "But didn't you just say—?" Let me explain. There are times when being alone is beneficial, it gives you time and space to reflect. But we are not meant to be alone ALL THE TIME. Life is challenging and I figured the reason God put so many humans in our lives is because we are supposed to lean on and help one another during those difficult times. The key of course, is choosing the RIGHT people to lean on so we don't have to meet life's challenges alone—reach out to someone for that support if and when needed.

Tales from the DEC

Even though I was a loner in school, I was the life of the party in my church community. I cannot explain the differences in attitude and circumstances where I was shunned in the daytime and a social butterfly in the evening. But what I do know is that I cherished those times that my church community embraced me in all my flaws and taught me to be a better person. Just imagine if I didn't have that community, what a different person I would be. Community is here for us if we just reach out to it. They can help us thrive and grow if we would only let them into our hearts and lives.

REPEAT AFTER ME (3 TIMES): <u>Sometimes it's good to be alone, but at other times I need community. I will find a supportive community.</u>

Q & A with DK

Q: Having others support you has to be somewhat challenging for people like yourself and others who have achieved so much because they were willing to do things alone and resist following a crowd. How do you reconcile this with the need for community?

A: It's quite simple. None of us, myself included, in fact did any of THIS on our own—our achievements, our goals, our success. No one. At times, we may have felt like we were alone, but just because someone wasn't physically present doesn't mean they weren't supporting us. So, none of our accomplished have really been made alone. We must realize humans are social by nature—just like animals that hunt together. We are drawn to other people, so I don't think it's genuine when people to say they don't need a community to achieve their dreams. You may not need community all the time, but no one is an island.

"Call to Action"

Do you have a community of people for your (1) spiritual (2) social (3) career (4) personal needs and wants? The great thing about community is everyone has a role. So—get to work finding a community to be connected!

God has a sense of humor.

He taught me

It was my last year of law school at the University of Georgia. I had a choice between taking criminal procedure (which EVERYONE told me to take, even though I knew I would NEVER try criminal law) and taking a 2nd securities law class, the type of law I practice now. However, these 2 class schedules conflicted and I was passionate about securities law so I knew I would get a better grade in that class. At that point, I was trying to keep my GPA above average, so I didn't take the criminal procedure class. Fast forward: I am the ranking Democrat on the Judiciary Non-civil committee which is the criminal law committee of the Georgia House of Representatives. In that committee, I've learned more than I ever could have in a criminal procedure class. I see you God.

Tales from the DEC

Apparently, someone told my parents I was a gifted child, so I took a test and, turns out, the state of Georgia agreed. I had always had an interest in math because of its certainty and unbiased answers. I was taking pre-algebra by the 7th grade. By the time I finished 12th grade Algebra III, (as well as years of Trigonometry, Geometry, and the like,) I thought I would never have to pull out another calculator for the rest of my life. Fast forward to law school, where I found myself taking MBA classes and eventually began living in excel charts most days. It just goes to show you, we can make plans but that doesn't mean they always work out the way we think they will.

REPEAT AFTER ME (3 TIMES): <u>I know what I would like to do in life, but I am also open and willing to follow where I am led.</u>

Q & A with DK

Q: Even if you don't like math as much as you did a child, is there anything you appreciate about math since you are around it so much in your career?

A: First let me say that the reason I don't like math as much as I did a girl is because I was made fun of for being smart and a math wiz so I lost an interest as a way to survive elementary school. It's unfortunate but that's the case for many young girls in America I think. But to answer your question, some people are under the illusion that because I have a master's in business administration, I somehow like numbers. Nothing could be further from the truth. I went to law school for the one very specific reason: I figured there would be little to no math. Well—God has a sense of humor because the area of law I practice involves lots of it. Not just any math either—the kind of math where a calculator won't do, you need a fancy excel formula to get it done. But I will say one of the things that I appreciate about numbers is that they don't lie. That's why with my investment advisory clients that are looking for wealth building, I always tell them to trust the numbers. 1 + 1 is always going to equal 2.

"Call to Action"

I would SERIOUSLY urge you to not cut anything or anyone out of your life completely, no matter how much you think it's useless now or hate it. Life has a funny way of recycling things in the most unexpected ways.

Others' mistakes are a real-life webinar.

Watch and learn

In life, my BEST teaching moments come when I am quiet, observing and learning from other people. There are so many people both succeeding and making mistakes along the way, their mistakes are the best teachers. You must observe and listen. What was the mistake they made? How did they overcome it? It doesn't have to be a formal sit-down discussion, you can learn a lot from people who are not famous or don't publicly tell their story when a mistake is made. We should never get so focused on our objectives that we think we can't make mistakes. Take time to be sensitive and learn when others fail.

Tales from the DEC

I used to skip Physiology class. The way it was set up at that time, class lasted an hour and a half with 30 minutes for lunch and 30 minutes for "study time." Well, I had the highest grade in the class and got an award for my work, so in my teenage mind, I figured that I could skip a portion of the class without getting into trouble. Turns out, I could not. Skipping was still not allowed, no matter what my grade was in the class. But here is the thing—I was not the only one skipping the class, but I was smarter about how I did it. The ones who got caught skipping were always very social, calling attention to themselves in the cafeteria. So, what did I do? I hid in back of the senior stage in the cafeteria and didn't draw any attention to myself. I never got caught.

REPEAT AFTER ME (3 TIMES): <u>I can and will learn from others in the hopes that I will not make the same mistakes they have.</u>

Q & A with DK

Q: I think it's important for those who have made mistakes to share their experience with others. It helps society become better and it's just a nice way to give back to others on similar paths. Why do you think there are not as many people sharing their struggles and mistakes?

A: Probably because our society highlights success stories a lot more than unsuccessful ones. We live in America, where the goal is to achieve the American dream and that's what we celebrate over and over again. We celebrate the end result and not the process. Think about it. This country is where dreams are supposed to come true, not nightmares. We need to create a space where it is ok to admit our mistakes without being judged for them, to create a narrative where we can learn from others. Without that, it will alway be more common to hear the success story than the unsuccessful story.

"Call to Action"

The next time someone makes a mistake on a path that you are currently on, I dare you to invite them to chat about it. Not only will you learn invaluable information, but it will be cathartic for them as well.

Life comes at you fast.

Life comes at you fast

In the fall of 2009, the law firm where I had been hired as the newest associate imploded. I was laid off. The next month, I started my current firm with the plan that I would do some work and get hired by another firm shortly after. As I said, it was 2009 and, surprise, that didn't happen. This series of events was FAR from the written timeline I had as a teenager. I wanted to make law partner by age 30 and then start my own business as a side hustle. This was NOT the way it was supposed to happen. It was scary and nerve-racking at the time, but you know what? It was the BEST way to become an entrepreneur, because I was forced to make plans and then when they didn't work out, POOF! I was an entrepreneur. Being an entrepreneur has made be a stronger person and allowed me to not only run for the Georgia House of Representatives, but to win at the age of 27. No law firm was going to let me miss work and do that.

Tales from the DEC

I have always had an entrepreneurial spirit. How could I not? I was raised by a family of entrepreneurs. Even as a kid, I was always finding ways to make extra money or to start a new initiative or project. I like the thrill of starting things from scratch and creating something special. It's not for everyone, but if you do have that entrepreneurial bug—run with it, foster it, embrace it, feed it. We need you in the world to bring innovation to our lives, and it starts with entrepreneurs taking those first steps. Dare to dream, because life is short and it comes at you fast, whether you are ready for it or not.

REPEAT AFTER ME (3 TIMES): <u>It's perfectly ok to accept a risky detour for my dreams.</u>

Q & A with DK

Q: Any regrets or things you would have done differently since it seems becoming a business owner did come at you rather unexpectedly?

A: I wish I had sought out a mentor and asked for help sooner. It is incredibly hard to start a business and it would have helped me to at least have a "life coach" encourage me when things got hard. Before I ordered one business card, I should have put a support system in place— family included— to prepare for what was to come. Even if you are not thinking of starting a business, getting a mentor is a good idea in general. It's certainly true when you undertake what I did, when I had planned something totally different for my life. It's never too early to seek out mentors to help you when life does come—and it comes fast.

"Call to Action"

In life, I have had some detours. This is how they have made me feel:

_____

_____

_____

_____

_____

_____

_____

Your destiny will find you.

Serendipity or Destiny

How did I become the 2nd youngest member of the Georgia legislature in 2011? I had a meeting planned with a state representative I had known from my time interning at the State House as a very young adult. We were supposed to meet on a Wednesday, but something came up and we moved to Thursday. Just so happens, two hours before I arrived for our rescheduled meeting, the predecessor in my seat decided to run for Governor of the State of Georgia. This wasn't pre-planned, no one knew about it and it caught his democratic colleagues off guard. Well folks, I just happened to be in his House district. I knew a good number of elected officials already, and I happened to be down at the Capitol for this rescheduled meeting, where sign-ups for the seat were taking place. True. Story. I was asked to run and here I am. This is the best example of destiny showing up that I can think of in the entire world.

Tales from the DEC

When I reflect on how shy I was in elementary school, it's amazing that I was ever noticed by anyone. I mean really, I cannot remember a time I spoke unless the teacher asked me a question. I have no idea why, but at Knollwood Elementary Schoo in Decatur, GA, the principal took a liking to me, so did my 4th grade teacher Ms. Howard. Together, they changed the trajectory of my life: First, they noticed I was gifted and so I was tested and was put into very exclusive, challenging classes in which I thrived because I worked better in smaller groups and I needed challenges to stimulate my mind. Second, they recommended that I become the student government representative for my grade. And well, as they say, the rest is history!

REPEAT AFTER ME (3 TIMES): <u>What is for me, I will receive. But it's up to me to be prepared to receive what is coming my way.</u>

Q & A with DK

Q: Is it as simple at being at the right place at the right time, or is there more to falling into your destiny like you did?

A: You also must be prepared to receive that destiny. At the time I was recruited, I didn't think I was prepared. I had just been laid off and was not only starting my own law firm (which I never wanted to do in life) but had also just started my MBA classes. But I had also already worked for two members of Congress, the Democratic Party of Georgia, founded a Young Democrats chapter at my university, and worked for a Committee Chairman for two years in the Georgia House of Representatives. Like a receiver in a football game, I was in position to receive what was in front of me because I was prepared, even if I didn't think so at the time.

"Call to Action"

What is your dream job or dream spouse or dream travel destination? If one of them was presented to youTODAY, would you be qualified and ready to receive it? If not, start on that path towards being able to receive that blessing.

Follow your passion, find your brand.

My adult passion

Whether you have read about my background or you are reading this because you know me personally, you know that I am passionate about capital markets—how money and wealth flows through the hands of individuals and businesses, particularly here in the United States. I didn't know the name of it when I was a teen, but I was always interested in HOW rich people became rich, not necessarily interested in WHO became rich (that came later and is critical to the discussion on generational wealth—another book I will write later). From there, I continued to learn more and more about capital, money and wealth, culminating into who I am today.

Tales from the DEC

From the time I was incredibly young, I had a passion for leadership—persuading others to believe and act towards a common goal. My senior year of high school, I organized a Senior picnic in your courtyard. It wasn't an official part of senior year and I was not an officer in the senior student council, but it was something I wanted to do and knew I could pull it off. So, I coordinated with student leaders and my mom and teachers and administration, and one sunny day there were Towers High seniors eating chicken wings and drinking sodas on the lawn of the senior courtyard. It was so successful; I was asked by my classmates to do it again. That's what happens when you are good at something, (which usually comes from being passionate about it)—people associate you with that thing.

REPEAT AFTER ME (3 TIMES): <u>My gifts will make room for me and enable me to follow my passion and attract opportunities to me.</u>

Q & A with DK

Q: Some people are a little wary of following their passion or telling their children to follow their passion in a capitalistic world. For example, if you have a passion for singing but can't sing, that's not going to bear much financial fruit for you. What do you about that?

A: That's very true! Listen, I am a very much a prag-matist. So, I do believe you have to find not only what you are passionate about but, realistically, what can ALSO make you money right? There are many a passionate people who cannot pay their bills throughout the world. But this chapter isn't about making money so much as it is about brand-ing. Even if you can't sing, if you are passionate about it, SOMEONE, SOMEWHERE will give you an opportunity to sing. I see it all the time. You might not get a standing ovation, but people love other passionate people, even if they don't share a calling. We have all seen it.

"Call to Action"

1. What are all the things I am passionate about?
2. Which of these things am I good at?
3. Which of these things can I monetize and make a living doing?

Whatever no. 3 is, do it NOW.

Momma knows best.

Tales from the DEC

My mom thinks that all her children are super heroes. And I know that if you are a mom reading this, you probably feel the same way about your child. But seriously my mom thought I could do anything and told me every chance I got that I could do anything I set my mind to accomplish. I have always been interested in government (surprise surprise) so she encouraged me to run a campaign for class president. I thought "I cannot get elected, what makes her think I can get appointed?" Long story short—I got the position and held it until I graduated. As usual, she knew best. Now I know someone reading this may not have the same family dynamics and awesome mom I had—but we all have someone we respect and can lean on to encourage us. Listen to that person. They want you to succeed.

REPEAT AFTER ME (3 TIMES): <u>I will listen to the wise</u> <u>words of someone I respect and trust; they can see</u> <u>greatness in me when I can't see it myself.</u>

Q & A with DK

Q: You were fortunate enough to grow up with two parents in your home and so you had an apparent role model to look up to in your mom. Not everyone is that lucky, so what are the characteristics of a person others should listen to?

A: That's very true. But remember that just because someone doesn't have a title, doesn't mean they aren't special in your life or family. So hopefully everyone has those people they can go to for advice. You can start with the circle of influence you have now and really think about who has your best interests at heart. If you don't already know that person, ask for help and you can get a sense of who is thoughtful about the advice they give you, then you can start to develop that relationship further.

"Call to Action"

Who in your life knows you better than anyone else? That's a perfect place to start when considering who to develop a deeper relationship with, or who you want to start one with in the first place. They will be invaluable on your journey called life.

Hard work will beat smarts and passion EVERY time.

Twice as hard!

I have a confession. I have had to fight twice as hard for everything that I have. I don't want people to look at my life now and imagine it's been this way the entire time. I made a decision early in life that if I wanted, I mean REALLY wanted, to realize my dreams that I had to work not only hard—but twice as hard to get what I wanted. I knew my smarts would only get me so far—passion was only going to get me started. Luckily, I had parents that were great examples and encouragers of this. So remember, no matter how smart or passionate you are, you still have to put in the WORK to see results. As with everything in life.

Tales from the DEC

It's no secret that some people are born with advantages that I and so many other people don't are not. But my parents instilled in me the value of hard work, because as a black female, it would take me working TWICE as hard as a white man to get what I wanted. My dad is the hardest working man I know, and my mom always required excellence. She knew excellence was the only way to compete against mediocre people with privilege. So it was drilled into all the Kendrick kids on a consistent basis that we had to not only get an education and do something we loved and were good at, but we had to work HARDER than anyone else. It's the lot we were dealt, but my mom made sure we didn't let it stop us.

REPEAT AFTER ME (3 TIMES): <u>I may not be the smartest, richest, or prettiest person in the room, but it will be darn hard to find someone who will outwork me.</u>

Q & A with DK

Q: How does this principle about hard work translate into the corporate world for you?

A: As an employer, I will tell you that I look for people who can get the job done. If you have a 2.0 and can get any task done, I will hire you. I don't let academics override someone who is passionate about the work I do or who has a "get it done" mindset. Imagine how many good people we miss by only looking at grades or test scores. Passion goes a long way in my industry, but you can be passionate and lazy at the same time—those two things aren't exclusive. I am always looking for someone with passion, some smarts, but most of all the tenacity to meet the objective, because I am a results-oriented person. Results matter most to me, and they're what should matter most to the rest of corporate America as well.

"Call to Action"

Print.

Hard work > Passion, Smarts or Beauty

It's up to us to make IT better.

What is "it"?

"It" is whatever it is that you think is not working according to how you think it should work. It could be government, your job, family life, your career, or anything else. Whatever that "it" is, I want you to know that you don't have to sit back and tolerate it. As a matter of fact, I am always advocating for the government to hold itself accountable, and for elected officials to advocate for changes that people want to see. I am a hard-liner in that sense, if you tell me you didn't vote, any complaint you have about government goes in one ear and right out the other. You didn't participate in the solution so that tells me it's not THAT big of a deal for you, you just want to complain. Advocacy is not something you can act on whenever you feel like it; advocacy and action have to be habitual and firm in order to get the results you desire. So—what are you going to do about it?

Tales from the DEC

Complaining about a situation was a "no go" in my family growing up. And let me tell you we had a lot of reason to complain. But instead of my parents complaining about this situation or another, they did something about it. Now that I think about it, I actually cannot remember one time in which my parents complained about something and didn't spur into action to do something about it—no matter if it was big or small, urgent or not—pointing out a problem and then doing something about it has always been their M.O. I am fortunate that they passed down that attitude of "do something about it" to their children. It has enabled me to not see myself as a victim, but rather a victor in any situation IF I execute a plan to change my situation.

REPEAT AFTER ME (3 TIMES): <u>I will make every effort to change the things I can instead of just complaining.</u>

Q & A with DK

Q: **This seems to be one of the biggest annoyances for you, particularly because you serve in government, which is all about advocacy and action right? How does one move from individual action towards collective action to provide and act on solutions?**

A: If you know me, you know one of my biggest pet peeves is people who complain without doing something about the issue. Nothing drives me more insane than people who have pity parties about something without any actionable items to rectify the situation. Remember our time on Earth is limited, it doesn't need to be spent simply complaining and not solving issues. So, if you are similar to me in that you believe complaining won't help solve an issue, I encourage you the next time someone is going down that path to say firmly "I understand. Now, what are we going to do about it?" You may lose some friends or not get invited to the pity parties, but I'm sure you'll be ok with that.

"Call to Action"

1. What is your "it"?

   _____

2. What can you do about "it"?

   _____

3. Will you do something about "it" EVERY DAY in EVERY WAY? (   ) Yes (   ) No

Excuses are not fallback plans.

An honest conversation with ourselves

When I reflect on why I convinced myself I could NOT do something, I found if I looked deep inside, it wasn't that I could NOT do something, it was that I just didn't WANT to do it. And we must own that. If you don't want to do something, just say that, not that you CANNOT do something. So, when a task or opportunity comes before me, I no longer question IF I can do something but if I WANT to do something, then I attribute it to my lack of motivation, not my lack of ability. It makes all the difference when we have those honest conversations with ourselves.

Tales from the DEC

My mom was a no excuses type of person. When we were asked to do something and we tried to give excuses for why it couldn't be done she would give me her usual "find a way" look that I can still see in my head to this day. Anytime I try to make an excuse about why I can't do something, I hear her voice in the back of my head saying, "Excuses only serve one person, the one who makes them." I had to learn to be resourceful at a young age because we didn't have much. But that didn't seem to stop my mom from expecting me to pull off the seemingly impossible. And by some miracle, I always did. I guess it's true what they say, kids rise to the expectations their parents set for them, so the bar should be high. I am not a parent, but it seemed to have worked for my mom.

REPEAT AFTER ME (3 TIMES): <u>Excuses may do me some good, but it won't do anything for others.</u>

Q & A with DK

Q: It seems like out of everything your parents taught you, the foundation of it starts with this concept that you can do anything you put your mind to, so no excuses. Work hard and get it done.

A: My parents were overly optimistic in their kid's abilities no matter what our circumstances and background were. I think people look at me now and think that for some reason, I just magically got here by my mom speaking positive affirmations over me, my dad working hard to provide for us and me doing the hard work. Let me be CLEAR: It took a lot of prayer, a lot of working hard to get access to resources and people that others naturally have access to by way of socioeconomic status, gender, race or background, and a lot of constant motivation. Others started at the 50-yard line with these same motivational principles, and I started out on the sidelines. But I have overcome a lot, and I owe that to my mom and dad.

"Call to Action"

The next time you are tempted to make an excuse about why you CANNOT do something, PAUSE and ask yourself: Is it that I CANNOT do this or that I do not WANT to? Be honest with yourself so you know how to move forward. It's ok if you don't want to do something.

I attract the energy I give out.

Karma

What goes around, comes around may be an ancient Hindu concept, but it is rooted in real life. Why people think they can treat people any kind of way and the universe won't see it is beyond me. You don't even have to believe in a higher being to know that Murphy's laws are real and that the Golden Rule is the standard for human behavior. We will all be on the opposite side of things eventually, so treat others with respect, as every human should be treated. I know it can be difficult sometimes, because there are some mean people in the world. I will be the first to admit I don't always follow my own advice, because there are hateful people in the political world. But I am striving every day to do better and I believe you are too.

Tales from the DEC

I will admit it. I was standoffish and defensive as a teenager. Not to make excuses, but you could hardly blame me. I had been severally bullied ever since elementary school, so why would I want to be anyone's friend or let down my guard? As you can imagine, there was no excuse for my behavior, so I spent four very lonely years in high school without many friends or people wanting to talk to me for fear of my quick temper and witty tongue. I had and still have an amazing ability to say something so witty that it hurts others feelings for a long time. In my lines of work, being standoffish can be detrimental, so I have now learned to moderate it. I am still a work in progress. I can still be a little more defensive than most people. It just goes to show, being bullied can have lifelong effects.

REPEAT AFTER ME (3 TIMES): <u>I will treat others as I want to be treated because the energy I give out is what I will receive.</u>

Q & A with DK

Q: We have all heard of karma and how it relates to the Golden rule. But can you give us a practical way to think about our actions that aren't so cliché and ancient?

A: Think of your actions as a boomerang. You throw something out there and you cannot be surprised if it returns to you. Instead of saying "karma is a b$*@&" or anything like that, just remember that our actions are boomerangs. I am always amazed at how brutally mean people can throw things out over and over again and they wonder what they are doing wrong or why they deserve tastes of their own medicine. You truly attract the energy that you give out—good or bad. We throw our actions towards others as boomerangs and they return to us in the same form.

"Call to Action"

This may be difficult, but the next time we are tempted to do something —in or out of character, but deep down we know it's not right,— ask yourself if you want this action to boomerang back to you. Choose your actions accordingly.

If no one is talking about you, you're doing something wrong.

Folks only talk about people who matter

Think about that. If you didn't matter, why would people spend time and energy to have a conversation and actually say your name? Now I won't go as far as some PR experts, who say "all PR is good PR," but I will say that there is something about people calling your name into the atmosphere that tells the universe you are important. You matter. Do we speak about people who don't matter? Nope. The more we matter, the higher our chances are that people will talk about us. So, if someone is talking about you, count it as a sign that you are doing something VERY right in life and that you matter. Remember, if no one is talking about you, you're probably doing something wrong.

If no one is talking about you, you're doing something wrong.

Tales from the DEC

When I would complain about classmates talking behind my back, my mom would always whip back in true Christian black momma fashion, "They talked about Jesus." As a teenager, this was super unhelpful because, at that stage in my development, I wanted sympathy, not Jesus, right? I didn't understand what my mom meant in its entirety until I became an adult. The ironic thing —or the thing I call "the boomerang effect"— was those same people who bullied me and couldn't seem to keep my name out of their mouth are the same ones that are mighty chatty with me now because of my position and network. Be careful how you treat people. The world is smaller and more interconnected than you think.

REPEAT AFTER ME (3 TIMES): <u>People only discuss people and things that matter; so, if I am being discussed, clearly, I matter.</u>

Q & A with DK

Q: Let's be honest. Some people are just mean and hateful and they are always going to be that way no matter how respectful you are to them. Particularly given your career in politics, how do you deal with it?

A: I mentioned this earlier in the book, but I have a gift of not caring. When I was growing up, my mom would say I had a "nonchalant attitude" and it infuriated her because I just let things go. But at times, this nonchalant attitude has served me well in adulthood, because I am particularly good at ignoring negativity. When you give things attention, not only do you throw fuel on a fire but you use some of your own energy. Like hours in a day, we have limited energy. I have made a choice to use that energy on positive and productive things, not negative and unproductive ones. And so, I have mastered the art of ignoring ignorance. I wish I could teach it. It's a peace like you have never known before.

"Call to Action"

Write down practical ways to ignore people talking about you. For example, when my social media gets crazy, I intentionally look for the supportive posts and respond to only those. It makes the posters I am ignoring furious— I don't have time for foolishness.

_____

_____

_____

_____

_____

_____

Nescrit cedere is what we should do.

"She who does not know how to give up."

This is what *nescrit cedere* means and it's the motto of my first college alma mater Oglethorpe University. How appropriate this is to sum up my life. For those of you reading this book, I can tell that this describes you as well. You have been met with difficult circumstances and times when you weren't sure you could make it, but here you are! You embody what James Oglethorpe did as he was trying to establish the university back in 1835. He didn't know how to give up, and neither should we.

Tales from the DEC

I graduated seventh in my high school class of over 200 students. But in the ninth grade, I didn't yet know I would succeed with such distinction. You see, I had to take Biology. I literally cannot tell you one other class in my high school career that was harder than Biology. I don't want to say I hated science, but I just didn't get it. I had a decent GPA, but this class was threatening to bring it down because I was barely getting a C. But, I persisted. Any time there was extra credit, Dar'shun did extra of the extra credit. Anytime there war an opportunity to spend extra time with the teacher or a tutor, I was right there. At the end of the day, I received a solid B, which felt like winning the lottery. My persistence paid off, short term and long term.

REPEAT AFTER ME (3 TIMES): <u>Giving up is not an option.</u>

Q & A with DK

Q: Life is filled with circumstances making it understandable to give up and no one would fault you. What are some practical tips for readers who don't want to give up? How can you encourage those people?

A: It's always important to remember your WHY. Your WHY can get you through some really hard times. So, whether its to support your family or make them proud or to make the world a better place or to show a naysayer you can do it, remembering that WHY can be the best motivation and adrenaline boost you could ever imagine. I would go so far as to recommend writing your WHY down or hang that picture of your family close by to remind you why you do what you do, even when things aren't so bad. You will be energized and perform better than before if you remember WHY you are doing what you are doing.

"Call to Action"

1. Task No. 1: _____. This is my WHY:

_____

_____

_____

2. Task No. 2: _____. This is my WHY:

_____

_____

_____

3. Task No. 3: _____. This is my WHY:

_____

_____

_____

"Stick" inspiration wherever you go.

A rainbow of notes

If you have ever been to any of my offices or to my home, you will see inspirational notes stuck everywhere! This is particularly true for my in-home office and library where there is a rainbow of sticky notes. It may not seem like it goes with the décor to have them everywhere, but let me tell you: when things get difficult, as they always eventually do, those sticky notes are a reminder of all the positivity I can create by changing my mindset and spurring myself into action. Our thoughts become our words that then become our actions. So, excuse my sticky notes while I go be positive and get some things done!

Tales from the DEC

I am not sure what age I started, but I have long kept a box of inspirational quotes. If I heard something inspirational, I would write it down on an index card and stick it in this box. Every morning, I would take an index card from the box and stick it on my mirror or carry it with me as my "inspirational quote of the day." So, when I was having a bad day or needed to inspire someone else, I could pull out a new inspirational quote. Positive affirmations are a key source of what helps me overcome trials and tribulations. Everyone must do what works for them. THAT worked for me and still does to this day.

REPEAT AFTER ME (3 TIMES): <u>I will find a way to stick close to my inspiration and remind myself that life is so full of hope and joy.</u>

Q & A with DK

Q: Whatever happened to that box of quotes? It seemed like you had accumulated a good deal of inspirational quotes over the course of several years.

A: Ha! I did. When I graduated from high school, I gave them to a young lady I was mentoring along with instructions on how to use them. I am not sure if she followed my instructions after I left for college, but that's the great thing about positive habits: You can pass them along and inspire other people. Imagine if we had a world that saw the glass half full instead of the other way around. So, whatever method you choose to uplift yourself, see if there is a way for you to pass it along. Spread the positivity! I have several inspirational journals now that I give to mentees at the end of the year, as well as boxes of quotes and thank you notes. Every day I write down 5 "blessings" in a book beside my bed. There is an awesome thing that happens when you INSIST on staying positive.

"Call to Action"

Get some sticky notes—all colors and sizes. Place them around your home or office. When you hear or see something inspirational, IMMEDIATELY write it down and stick it somewhere nearby. Watch your attitude change as you reflect on these quotes.

Love your Mondays!

Change your view of Mondays

I read somewhere that most heart attacks happen on Mondays. Why? It's because people are overworked, stressed and anxious about a new week. I mean WOW! That's a whole other book to write. But for the purposes of this book, let's change our perspective on what Monday means. For me, Monday marks the beginning of a new week of opportunities. Will there be challenges? Of course. But we are all superheroes who can take on anything with preparation and a good attitude. I jump out of bed early on Mondays (and every other day) excited about what the day may bring that might change the trajectory of my life. Changing your mindset is not only good for your mental health, but your physical health as well.

Tales from the DEC

As you can imagine, I had to work up to liking Mondays (and mornings). I used to think of days as just that—days. I would wake up to go to school Monday through Friday and just going through the motions. I guess it was better than dreading Mondays, but life is too short to just exist. I wanted to be excited about each day, particularly the start of a work week. So, I had to slowly develop the habit of looking forward to Mondays and celebrating all that a work week could be. If you think about it, something can happen this week to change your life forever. Be excited about that! Expect good things to happen to you! Now, developing this mindset wasn't easy, particularly when I knew there would be a challenge in the coming week. But going from simply existing on Mondays to thriving on Mondays is a change of pace I ASSURE you will love.

REPEAT AFTER ME (3 TIMES): Mondays are the beginning of a new week, an opportunity to show the world what I am made of, so I will get EXCITED about Mondays!

Q & A with DK

Q: **You must be really excited about life in general, because I don't know anyone who gets up as early as you do every day—including weekends,**

holidays and vacations. Is it just motivation that causes you to muster the energy and discipline to get up so early every day?

A: Well, it's motivation for sure, but there is also a practical side to getting up early, which is why I have a 5:00 a.m. rise time EVERY day. Mornings are my best opportunities to get and stay motivated. Knowing every day is a gift from God and an opportunity to thrive will get you out of bed, but what will sustain you throughout the day is the time you'll have when the world isn't up and there are no distractions. I can meditate, pray, recite my affirmations in total peace, write the quote of the day on my board and think about how I will handle the day ahead. Because there are no distractions, I get most of my important work done and still have time to exercise, which is vitally important to this whole positivity concept I am pushing in this book. So yes, I have lots of reasons to like Mondays and to love early mornings.

"Call to Action"

I understand not everyone is a morning person, particularly early mornings. But find that time to set aside, ideally BEFORE your day is in full swing, to prepare your mind, body, and soul for the day. Write it here.

This is the time EVERYDAY that I will prepare my mind, body, and soul to take on the day with positive affirmations and focus:

Change the font.

A change of scenery

I have several "work areas" set up all over my house. I even have a table outside overlooking the back yard. Why? Because I am a big believer that we can think more clearly and more creatively when we simply change our scenery. I believe this so much that when I am writing something that will take a while to get done (like this book), I will even change the font several times. It may not seem like a big deal, but sometimes we just need something different to inspire us. This concept can be applied to life and business in general. Want to see a different perspective? Change the font.

Tales from the DEC

My mom will tell you that I was a very precocious child. A teacher once told her that she had to keep me busy because, if she didn't, I would get in trouble because I was always looking for a new challenge. It turns out that is STILL very much true today, which is why I always have several projects going on at any time. When my mom got this advice, she tried to put me in every activity under the sun. Can you imagine me as a baton twirler? Yeah, me either, which is why I didn't last long. Girl Scout? That would be a hard pass. But I did enjoy my time as a cheerleader while I was studying to play Mary in an upcoming Christmas play while I was serving on student government in school and singing in the church choir. My mom became a master at changing the font for me and it kept me out of trouble and allowed me to be creative and find my talents.

REPEAT AFTER ME (3 TIMES): <u>I am not a tree. If I don't like where I am, I can move.</u>

Q & A with DK

Q: It's hard to imagine little changes like working from another place in your house or changing the font of a document can have so much affect on spurring inspiration. Are there larger scale changes that inspire you as well?

A: Oh yes! Every time I get a call or note or email from someone that says "Thank you for helping me with…" I get inspired all over again to continue the work I do. Knowing I am making a difference in the lives of others is the best way to stay inspired, even if I am never acknowledged for it. I highly suggest that you find little ways to inspire yourself every day, but for those LARGE hits of inspiration and creativity, help someone that can never repay you or more than likely will never say "thank you." If that doesn't lift you up, I am not sure what will.

"Call to Action"

When do I feel MOST inspired by? (record for a week) How can I incorporate that into what I do daily, weekly, monthly and throughout the year?

_____
_____
_____
_____
_____
_____
_____
_____
_____
_____
_____
_____
_____
_____

Strive to do what lasts.

Power is temporary; influence is forever

I was Student Body President my last year of college (shocker, right?) As Student Body President, I implemented, for the first time ever, office hours thirty minutes a week for each member of student government. First, I had to secure an office with materials and a computer, because we didn't even have that. Second, I set up a recurring schedule and published it so that students knew when they could stop by and get information and ask for help. Fast forward to 2019, a few administrations after my implementation: I was back on campus for Alumni week and volunteering for a project when a student said, "Hey! I have to leave for OSA [which is what we called Oglethorpe University's student government] office hours." You should have seen the smile that came over my face. I didn't say anything, but you would have thought I had won the lottery. That should be the goal—leaving a positive legacy that lasts.

Tales from the DEC

This is an embarrassing admission, so bear with me as I try to sound like an adult. When I was a kid, I had an enormous amount of influence over other kids at my church. So, I decided in elementary school to give everyone nicknames based on convenience store candy (I told you this was silly). Anyway, a church friend was trying to describe someone we had grown up with who had a nickname. They said, "You know, we called him icee." And I immediately knew who they were talking about. Why they remembered that is beyond me. I tried to forget how I was too creative for my own good at that time (what an imagination to name kids after convenience store snacks---it's embarrassing). The most positive thing that came out of that dialogue was proof that someone had been listening, and that I'd had enough influence to make a silly nickname last all these years.

REPEAT AFTER ME (3 TIMES): I don't have to use power to influence others; I can use my leadership.

Q & A with DK

Q: **You had to develop as a leader and distinguish between power and influence. A lot of people think they are the same thing. Was there an "a-ha" moment for you when you figured out the difference?**

A: Actually, there was. It really hit me when I was elected to the Georgia House of Representatives. At the time, my party was in the super minority, so we had NO power. Over the next few years, since I had no substantive power, I had to use my powers of persuasion to get things done for my district and constituents. And then it hit me: even though I had a title, it was powerless in the grand scheme of Georgia politics. I was able to be productive by using my talents of persuasion to get things done. So, influence is never solely about a title or fame or fortune, it's about how you can persuade others to believe in whatever it is you do.

"Call to Action"- Print.

> I will strive to leave a positive legacy on this Earth every day.

Follow up to follow through.

The art of the follow up

Ladies and gentlemen, I present the name of one of my future books: The Art of the Follow-Up. You may be asking why I need to write a whole book about following up. It's because, for some reason, people don't realize how important it is to get to the goal. I am shocked by how many people in business don't follow up after an event or email or phone call. We live in a world that is constantly giving us information about new things to try and what to spend money on or who the next big star will be. If we don't follow up on things that could help us reach our goals, we will never manifest our dreams. We must be able to recognize opportunities and figure out ways to follow up with specific deadlines to do so. Do, follow up, rinse, repeat. Make it a habit, turn following up into an art form.

Tales from the DEC

As you can imagine, I was persistent as a youth. If my parents made me any promises, I would follow up right after I had done my side of the deal. My member of Congress once came to speak with my eighth grade civics class and knew immediately that I wanted to have a career in politics. So, my last year of high school, I called her District office and told them I wanted to be an intern. I followed up day after day and got to the point where I insisted I would be showing up first thing when the summer started. Long story short: I showed up and worked the entire summer for my then Member of Congress. As they say, the squeaky wheel gets heard. If you don't follow up, someone else will.

REPEAT AFTER ME (3 TIMES): <u>If I see an opportunity, I will follow up and act within 3 days.</u>

Q & A with DK

Q: Some people believe if someone wants something bad enough or if you are that valuable, people will follow up with you. How do you respond to that?

A: One, it's pretty arrogant to think you are so special that people will chase you down after any interaction with you. I mean, I guess there are some folks like Oprah who got it like that, but I have yet to meet one person who is like Oprah. Not following up is like someone extending their hand to you and you just turn and walk away. Not only is it rude, but that handshake (follow-up) provides something tangible and real in a world that is FILLED with distractions. What will differentiate you as a person or business is going to be your ability to recognize a hand being extended and to follow up and shake that hand, (while slipping a business card to the other person). The early bird may get the worm, but only if they follow up on the invitation to get up early.

"Call to Action"

Take out a sticky note and write somewhere near your planner or computer or nightstand or all three and write the words "FOLLOW UP." Let this be a reminder that whoever you met or whatever opportunity you saw throughout the day, it is your OBLIGATION to follow up within three days.

Service should be our ultimate life objective.

Why service? Let me explain

Each of us has SOMETHING that is unique to the world and that we need to share with others. When I speak about service, a lot of the time people think I am talking about something large scale and expensive or time consuming. Maybe you think I am talking about a title or position. Service can be calling to check on a friend, or writing a thank you note to a colleague, or babysitting your nieces and nephews for a few hours. We must change what it means to "serve" into something practical that is not just for millionaires, elected officials and philanthropists. If you see someone in need, ask yourself if you can help. Now, you cannot help everyone, but those you can help, should be helped. That is service. It's the smallest thing we can do to make the world a better place, because we all need help at some point.

Tales from the DEC

You know who is the ULTIMATE servant to me (besides Jesus of course)? My mom. Let me tell ya'll something: If there was a dictionary with pictures of people beside the words, my mom's picture would be right there along with my dad's right next to the word "servant." Those two people are the epitome of true service to others. Growing up, I watched them serve diligently, faithfully, and happily in our church and community. I didn't understand why they gave so much to people they didn't know and to so many causes they didn't get paid for. I admit I even got angry about it sometimes, because it took their time, money, resources and attention away from us and I sometimes felt cheated. But NOW—NOW I get it. Their example of what it means to serve is ingrained in me, and it will never go away.

REPEAT AFTER ME (3 TIMES): <u>I cannot help everyone. But to those I can help, I will give what I can.</u>

Q & A with DK

Q: It's obvious that your parents' service to others had a profound affect on you because of the particular career path you have chosen. What recommendations would you give to other parents?

A: My advice would be this: Your kids are watching. I am not a parent but I think it's very true that kids watch what you do and listen to what you say even when you think they are not. I don't say this lightly and I believe it with 100 percent of my heart and soul: The reason that I am so blessed is because when I was going up my parents planted in me the seeds of sacrifice and service. I honestly believe that. They didn't know they were doing it at the time, but I believe it to be true. So parents, plant those seeds in your children. Show them what it means to be a selfless human being. I promise you, when they are older, they will not forget it and you will have raised another giver in the world—because Lord knows we have enough takers.

"Call to Action"- Fill in the blank.

1. I can serve DAILY by _____
   _____.

2. I can serve WEEKLY by _____
   _____.

3. I can serve MONTHLY by _____
   _____.

4. I can serve YEARLY by _____
   _____.

Know thyself—and know of others.

Trust but verify

We have all heard the phrase "Know thyself," right? I mean truly knowing what your strengths are and magnifying those while also knowing your weaknesses and downplaying them. But there is a second part of knowing yourself and that is to know—I mean really KNOW—others as well. That's why relationships and spending time with people either personally or professionally is so important. You cannot get to know someone you barely talk to or spend no time with. It becomes even more important if you are relying on others to make a decision. You have to find what works for those you are trying to cultivate a relationship with, BUT; the important thing is that the relationship is moving forward to a place of respect and trust.

Tales from the DEC

Like any other child perhaps, I loved playing in the water when I was young. On a trip to White Water for summer camp as a child, I decided to climb onto these plastic lily pads where the water was about seven feet deep. I was nine years old, and I didn't realize how deep the water was so I asked a friend if I could touch the bottom at barely five feet. She said yes. Well, onto the lily pads I went and to the bottom of the pool I sank. I was rescued by a lifeguard and out of utter embarrassment turned the brightest red any little black girl could. My friend ran over to me to make sure I was ok and I gave her the meanest look I could at the time. But I learned a very important lesson that day: Know what I can do and KNOW if others know what they are talking about before diving in the deep end.

REPEAT AFTER ME (3 TIMES): <u>I will get to know myself more and more and I will do the same for others around me.</u>

Q & A with DK

Q: Do you consider yourself a good judge of character once you get to know someone?

A: It depends. I know that's a non-answer, but it's true. I think I am more likely to discern someone's spirit and motives if I am at a point in my life where things are good and calm and stable.

There have been other times in my life where things have been disappointing and rocky, and I think those were the times I let bad people into my life. Now luckily, as with most things, when I am out of those dark places, a light is shone on the people I don't need in my life and I am able to distance myself from them. And I am not one of those people who judges anyone's character to the extent that they must be perfect for them to be in my circle. Lord knows I am FAR from perfect. I am still a work in progress, however; I am always looking for people to complement my strengths or fill in my shortcomings. Those are the people that I am naturally drawn to and it's served me pretty well in the past.

"Call to Action"

Every person in your life should have a role that enhances your life in some way. Make a list of your ten closest people in life and list their roles and how they make your life BETTER. If you can't list the HOW they make your life better, you may want to seriously consider the extent to which they play a part in your life.

You'll know when it's time to move on.

The "Effective" Test

Whenever I am involved with a project or serving on a board or counseling someone, I give myself a litmus test to tell when it's time to move on. This is the question I ask myself: Am I being effective? Period. If the answer is "no," it's time to move on. If the answer is "yes," I consider remaining involved. I believe that one of the biggest problems in politics is that people want to stay where they are for eternity even if their prime time has come and gone and gone even further. We must know when to let go and move on to bigger and better things. I am not saying it will be easy, and you may shed some tears and even have some initial regrets, but if I can't be effective at what I am doing—why would I continue to do it when someone else CAN be effective? Staying in a place I no longer belong when others can do the job is just selfish in my opinion.

Tales from the DEC

I was Beta Club President my senior year of high school (How I became President is a whole other book). Beta Club was supposed to be an academic organization that did service projects. That is what it was SUPPOSED to be. So, I planned any number of service projects for us seniors to do throughout our term. Very few showed up, even though service hours were a requirement for staying a Beta club member. About three months to the end of my term and senior year, I gave up. I'll admit it. I decided to focus my attentions on getting financial aid to attend college and preparing myself mentally for my college experience. Sometimes we try as hard as we can, but it just doesn't work. I moved on. Happy I did, too. I don't see it as a failure or me being a quitter. The reality was that it was time to focus on other priorities. I have no regrets.

REPEAT AFTER ME (3 TIMES): <u>When I know it's time to move on, I will have the courage to take that step.</u>

Q & A with DK

Q: What's your best "it's time to move on" moment?

A: Well, I think that has yet to be seen, but to date, my best "it's time to move on" moment came in college when I was Secretary of a certain organization. So, I take any role I am elected or appointed to very seriously. If you don't want me to do my job, you shouldn't hire me. Period. Long story short, the executive board never let me help them set agendas for meetings (and y'all KNOW I don't do "free for all" meetings) and didn't appreciate or even read my meeting minutes. So, I turned in my resignation as Secretary after one semester. I knew even at that young age that my time was valuable and if others didn't value my time, there was no use in me having a title just to have it. It was time to put that energy and skill into other organizations and interests I had, like student government. The great thing was, I got support from others who saw what I was trying to do and respected that I knew it was time to move on.

"Call to Action"

Take some time to list all the activities and things that you do. Now, have an honest conversation with yourself about your effectiveness. Rank yourself on a scale of 1 to 5 for each of these activities. I highly suggest you consider getting rid of everything that is NOT a 4 on the way to a 5.

I own several shades of lipstick.

Let me explain

When I say I own several shades of lipstick, what I mean is that I have an ability to adapt to any situation because I am flexible. Now, this is a trait that I had to learn and really train myself to do, because Type A personalities like stability and don't really like change. We like consistency and predictability, so flexibility was not a part of my life plan. I had to force myself to go into situations with an open mind, because if there's one thing we can all learn pretty fast, it's that nothing is constant; change is inevitable. Now this doesn't mean I let go of my morals, principles or objectives, but maybe the process for achieving my objectives has to change or a compromise must be made to get things done. This ability to adapt will get you more invitations, more responsibility, and more opportunities to shine. Trust me.

Tales from the DEC

I have a confession. I have had the sleep habits of an old woman my whole life. I have always been an early riser and early to bed. I believe this comes from my dad's side of the family, because my aunt and grandma are the same way. One day my church took a teen trip to Florida as we did almost every year. Due to excitement or adrenaline or whatever it was, this two day trip turned into twenty-four hours of no sleep. Could I have gone to my bunk and slept? Yes. But then I would have missed the late-night walk on the beach and the card games and the interesting talks amongst all the teenagers and friends. I wasn't happy about the lack of sleep (and slept for almost twenty-four hours after), but it was worth adapting to an unfamiliar and unexpected situation to create those memories.

REPEAT AFTER ME (3 TIMES): <u>There is no situation that will catch me off guard, because I will always be prepared to adapt if necessary.</u>

Q & A with DK

Q: Most men obviously don't wear lipstick. You got a saying for them? Do you think it's easier for men or women to adapt?

A: Yes, of course I do. For men, the saying is "I have several ties I can wear," or the original saying "I wear many hats." The concept is still the same.

I do believe it's easier for women to adapt, because we have to all the time. It's not like we have the same respect level or power placement most men receive automatically in any situation. So, we adapt based on where we are with people at the time and the situation we walk into at any given moment. Plus, I must personally say that I have seen more women than men jungle multiple things simultaneously. So, I think women have a natural talent for doing many things at a time and adapting their behaviors based on the task that needs to be completed.

"Call to Action"

How can you be flexible in a situation without being run over— which is common among women who often bend too much to avoid conflict? Write down your thoughts, and the next time you have something to do with others, implement your plan. You can revise your plan as needed.

Giving up is a waste of time.

How so?

Giving up is a waste of time because time goes on, whether you are working on a goal or not. In high school, I knew I wanted to be a lawyer and I initially thought "Ugh. It's going to take seven years. I will be X years old." But the more I thought about it, seven years would pass and I would be the same age whether I had a law degree or not. The reason I think giving up is a time waster can be explained in these two scenarios:

1. If you give up then decide to go back to working on that goal, you would have missed that much more lead time.
2. Even if you decide to never go back to working on that goal, the time that you wasted on the goal leaves you with nothing to show for it. So, presented with these two scenarios that are both time wasters, why not adjust the HOW you get to your goal instead of giving up altogether?

Tales from the DEC

In high school, I oversaw high school spirit week as Spirit and Pride Chair. My first year, I came up with the idea to make over 1,000 handmade basketballs and tape them to the high school walls in different graduation years. Talk about crazy! It sounded like a good idea at the time, but as I was on my 300th handmade construction paper basketball, I really wanted to just order some orange basketballs and stick them up on the wall, in no particular shape or form. But I thought it would be a nice touch, so I completed those 1000 handmade basketballs and put them up as numbers on the wall. When spirit week came, they were a BIG hit. I still don't think anyone knew who did it, but I was so proud seeing star athletes walking around with them on and seeing them taped to our senior year memory books.

REPEAT AFTER ME (3 TIMES): <u>Giving up is a waste of time. The time will go by anyway so may as well use it toward my goal.</u>

Q & A with DK

Q: Ok, we need some clarification, because some things people need to give up. There must be a time when we know what our limits are and take our losses so we can move on to other things that give us a better chance of being successful.

A: That is true, however I find that my biggest break-throughs come right after I have decided to keep going after a big disappointment. And I believe a lot of breakthroughs are immediately on the other side of very tough times. So, I don't want to encourage people to give up when they want to, because we all have wanted to quit, but I understand every situation is different. What I would encourage people to do is know their situation, ask for professional help to truly assess if something isn't working, determine if there is a way to pivot, so you can change how you reach your goal and not give up entirely. Make the decision as quickly as possible, to save as much time as possible.

"Call to Action"

Current Project/Task	How is it going? (Good/Bad)	What can I change before giving up?

Systems spur success systematically.

That's what it's called!

It wasn't until I was getting my MBA that I had a word for what I have been doing my entire life. Systems: a consistent, repeated way of doing something. I am one of the most predictable people you will ever meet, which has served me well in some instances because I am very disciplined. But it has also turned out to be a struggle, as spontaneity is still a very hard concept for me. One of the reasons that I am a BIG fan of putting systems in place in our lives is the more you do something the same way, the better you get it at. Practice makes perfect, right? I have mastered my morning routine as a system because I have been doing it consistently for the last ten years. Now I know it's hard for some people to get into a routine, but I encourage you to try to put in place at least one system in your life. Try it out! You may like it.

Tales from the DEC

My mom required that we make our bed every day. I didn't question why. It was just one of her rules. One day, I was rushing out of the house for something and I left my bed unmade. I knew I would get in trouble for it, but I literally had no time and had to be somewhere (and you all know how I am about being on time). I remember that particular day was rough at school, not because of others, but because my whole attitude was just depressing for some reason. As soon as I got home, out of habit, I made my bed. You would be surprised how my attitude improved. I am convinced it's because my system was broken that morning and psychologically my mind and body responded, sensing something hadn't been done. I can tell you that to this day, the ONLY time my bed isn't made is when I am deathly sick, and even then, I manage to at least put the decorative pillows on the bed.

REPEAT AFTER ME (3 TIMES): <u>I will form productive and healthy habits that will propel me on my path to success.</u>

Q & A with DK

Q: Come on DK. Does making your bed REALLY have that drastic an effect on someone's attitude?

A: I don't know. All I can tell you is the effect it has on me, even to this day. I have been doing the same routine so long that if I miss a step, my whole day feels off until I go back and complete the task. I mean, some people like randomness and if it works for them, I say go for it. But I believe you can only truly master something unless you do it consistently the same way every day. The good habits that I have formed didn't come by doing them when I felt like it or sporadically but by intentionally creating systems in my life that support the work that I am doing. I mean we truly all have systems in our lives even though we may not call or recognize them as such. All I am saying is, since you have systems anyway, incorporate new ones that you want to master in order to keep you focused and in the best position to accomplish your heart's desires.

"Call to Action"

1. Describe areas of your life where you think you could be more efficient.
2. Describe things you could do on a consistent basis to be more effective in that area of your life.
3. Do it and record your results for one month, adjusting as necessary.

Stand for SOMETHING...
and bring a cane.

Stand for SOMETHING revisited

We have all heard the saying of "stand for something or you will fall for anything." In this day and age, we need to revise that to be CLEAR that the purpose of that saying was to encourage people to stand for something they believe in that is good and positive. I mean, Hitler certainly stood for something, so it's important to put this saying in context. Unfortunately, I had to make this distinction because people will take my words and twist them in the strangest and most evil ways. Stand for something you believe in that's not racist, sexist, homophobic, anti-Semitic, etc.—hopefully you get the point. I know none of you reading this book ever would take my words out of context, but just in case this book gets in the hands of someone different than you and I.

Tales from the DEC

My mom has been accused of making me too independent, and I have been accused of being too independent. Not quite sure what is meant by that, but I will take that over the alternative. You see, my mom was raised briefly in the foster care system. But even growing up, she realized that education was the pathway to a better life. And as a black girl, I was always warned (and it turned out to be absolutely true) that I had to try and accomplish twice as many things to be considered even remotely competitive in this world. And my mom made sure that when I stood for what I believed, I brought a big stick with me. A stick of education, a stick of facts, a stick of tenacity and perseverance—never empty handed and always prepared. She is one smart cookie, and I am lucky to have her.

REPEAT AFTER ME (3 TIMES): <u>I can and will stand for something that helps not only me, but my fellow human race.</u>

Q & A with DK

Q: Do you have a recent memory of standing up for something—with a cane?

A: I have many in my political life, but that's reserved for a subsequent book. Let me give you an example from my mom: She wanted to be an accountant, but surprise!— God blessed her with me at not the most convenient time, so she held off. Fast forward to 2011, I had just graduated with my fourth degree. My mom decided to enroll in school to get her Associate's in project management. She had to get back into the swing of things being out of school for so long, working a full-time job and helping with grandkids. At any point, we would not have blamed her for giving up her dream of getting a college degree, but she didn't. And December of 2013 was one of the proudest moments of my life, because the very thing she stood on—education—she finally achieved. Ok, now I am tearing up.

"Call to Action"

What are you willing to DIE for? Is it family? An issue? A person? Everyone should have that ONE thing. What is yours?

There is no leadership without service.

"Servant leadership" is redundant

Leadership without service is not leadership, it's someone holding a title. Nothing frustrates me more than the person who is in a position of leadership and doesn't understand that their first priority is to SERVE those whom they lead. Leadership isn't about power or self-service or having others serve you, it is about being able to communicate a vision for the people you serve and persuading them to follow you to accomplish that vision. As the saying goes, "If you are a leader and no one is following you, you're not a leader; you're just out for a walk." How do you get others to follow you willingly? You get to know their needs and serve them. I am on a one-woman crusade to get people to stop calling actions "servant leadership," because it's just leadership. There is leadership without service, so no need for the adjective.

Tales from the DEC

I mentioned this in a previous chapter, but if there was a dictionary with a picture next to the word "service," my parents would be right there. Growing up in the church, they are some of the hardest working servants of God I have ever seen. They served diligently, sacrificially, uncomplainingly, joyfully and they embodied every other trait of a true servant. Unbeknownst to them, I watched and admired them from the time I was ten years old. They didn't serve for recognition or to get something out of it, but in the purest and most selfless form I have ever witnessed here on Earth. They taught us Kendrick kids at a young age what it TRULY means to serve, with or without a title. They were able to lead a group of people to execute the vision they had for their ministry through service and love. I believe they are perfect examples of leadership.

REPEAT AFTER ME (3 TIMES): <u>I am not a leader if I am not serving.</u>

Q & A with DK

Q: Everyone knows there are courses and books and whole degree programs on servant leadership. Go into more detail on why the concept of "servant leadership" doesn't make sense to you.

A: Does "wet water" or "dead corpse" or "Christian Baptist" make sense? Sometimes I think we, as people, try to sound more sophisticated than we need to be, which makes understanding concepts harder than it needs to be. Being the practical person I am, I use as few words as I can in general. Since it's redundant to say, "lit light" or "hot fire", why would I accept that "servant leadership" is a thing based on my previous argument. Just say "leadership." That word should encompass all the traits we think about when we think about leaders, INCLUDING— and ESPECIALLY— the fact that it is a service position.

"Call to Action"

1. What positions of power do you hold, either with or without a title?
2. How do you use your position to SERVE others?
3. Is it true service or service with an ulterior motive?
4. How can you improve on your SERVICE to others?

Appendix-
My Morning Routine

4:45 am-   Wake up and "weigh in" on my scale

5:47 am-   Say my morning affirmations (see preamble)

5:50 am-   Go into my closet and pray and listen to God's instructions for the day

5:05 am-   Make bed and go to office to prep coffee, write another inspiration on my white board and turn on computer

5:10 am-   Take my dog Dezzy out to use the restroom, fix her food and cut cut on lights downstairs--plan meals for the day

5:20 am-   Brew coffee and read aloud more positive affirmations from my calendar and sticky notes

5:27 am- Post my #MorningMotivation from #DarshunSpeaks on all social media

5:30 am- Start my "morning routine" checklist

5:45 am- My dad calls

6:00 am- I plan my day in 15 minute increments, highlighting priorites and the ONE thing today I will do that scares me

6:30 am- Read and meditate in my Bible

7:00 am- Exercise: Rotation of cardio, weights and yoga

7:30 am- Breakfast

8:00 am- Get ready for the day...even if I have NO WHERE to go

9:00 am- Read a book for 1 hour

10 am- Back in the home office for the rest of the day

Appendix- My 10 Most Used Inspirational Thoughts

1. I am the only one ultimately responsible for my fate.
2. I am enough! Enough is what I need, enough is what I have, I am more than enough.
3. I will exercise my faith in a limitless God daily.
4. Everything happens at the time it should and not a moment too late or early.
5. We are only here (on Earth) for a little while; let's make the most of it.
6. Service is what I do; if I am not serving, I am not living.
7. I can and I will. Period.
8. Giving up is not an option.
9. I persist.
10. As long as God still reigns, everything will be ok.

CPSIA information can be obtained
at www.ICGtesting.com
Printed in the USA
FSHW021605160521